Taming the Terrible Twos:

A Parent's Survival Guide

By Ann Marie Dwyer

ISBN-10: 1478234458
ISBN-13: 978-148234456
LCCN: 2012913050

The Terrible Twos are a bittersweet time for toddlers and parents: both too long and too short...but either way, completely survivable. Learn from parents who have been there.

From what toddlers understand to how to get them to talk to you and from managing defiance to keeping them happy and healthy, everything you need to survive the Terrible Twos is right here.

Find out how much your toddler's behavior will predict how he will act as a teenager. Teach him to make good decisions, take on responsibility and cope with new siblings and friends. Conquer sharing, hair pulling and tantrums at the mall. Along the way, learn to laugh at the amazing things this little person does right before your eyes.

Table of Contents

Acknowledgements

Edited by John McDevitt
Layout Design by
Linda Valentine-Dean

Guest Articles:

John McDevitt
Barbara Whitlock

Testimonials:

Melanie Denyer
Tina Hartley
John McDevitt
Barbara Whitlock

Cover Art Photography:

John McDevitt

Poem from Foreward by
Ann Marie Dwyer

Foreward

I have been here before.
Yesterday, you were my baby,
But today you are terrible,
My two-year-old chore.

A litany of "No-No-No"
Streams from my mouth
And ironically from yours
While we are both on the go.

"Ten hours of sleep,"
I read somewhere,
What a crock!
Written by a creep

Who never had a little one
With an ice-pop and fish crackers,
Grilled cheese and peanut butter,
But still was not done.

Nursery rhymes and the potty train.
Picassoesque drawings,
With wallpaper frames.
Certainly, I am insane.

But then I see how proud you are,
Magic marker streaks and
Water color spots,
My little budding artist star!

I hold you close to me.
Silently, I thankfully pray,
"This time is so short,
For soon, you will be three."

In your parenting journey, you have already encountered surprises no class or book would ever have prepared you to see or survive. Throughout the chapters which follow, I will take you through the life of Terry, a Terrible Two. We will take a few detours from some parents I know who have survived this childhood stage which makes us understand why some species eat their young. In the end, you will hear success stories which will warm your heart with the faith Terrible Twos are survivable.

From these testimonies, you will find a familiar thread: Surviving the terrible twos prepares you for surviving teenagers. You may just find yourself returning to this book a decade from now and finding some wisdom yet again.

During the editing phase of this book, two schools of thought arose. The first suggested Chapter 5 (Managing Defiance) should be the first chapter. The second (and prevailing) led to the design you will find in the Table of Contents. Learning about why your toddler acts the way he does may just make Chapter 5 useful for when you keep other people's toddlers.

What I learned was, the first school of thought was populated by those without toddlers or who had only experienced the Terrible Twos in department stores or restaurants.

If you come to this book with preconceived notions as to what the Terrible Twos have in store, I only ask that you set them aside to read this book. This year (ish) holds a wonderful experience for you and your toddler. Open your eyes and your mind to what he is seeing for the first time. Terry has a lot to teach you.

Chapter 1

What makes them tick?

Toddlers are brilliant little people. They have gone beyond the baby stage and are mobile. Their inquisitive nature is pervasive. With a thirst for knowledge and a sponge-like brain to soak up the world around them, toddlers are the best learners. Parents marvel at the changes in their children between birth and walking. It pales in comparison to the changes which follow.

In the time lovingly referred to as the Terrible Twos, your baby will grow into a talking, running, playing, pretending, mimicking personality. Character is developing. New emotions, both good and bad, emerge for the first time. The seeds of right and wrong sprout. Discovery is around every corner, inside every box and under everything. The child's independence is born. Indeed, it is a wondrous time.

Terrible?

Why is it called terrible? Experiments often fail the first time. Failure is a difficult emotion: even for adults and especially the adults who witness a child's failure. Parents must separate themselves from their children, allowing their toddlers to make mistakes. Each mistake is an opportunity to learn, grow and build character.

Change is hard, even as a child. Before children can adequately express themselves in language which parents understand, they revert to babyish methods to vent their frustrations. Tantrums, whining and mildly aggressive behaviors, like biting and hair pulling, become the expression of emotion. Parents are comforted in the knowledge that this memorable time does come to an end.

Terrible, too, is the parent's loss of a baby. While your child was totally dependent on you, seemingly yesterday, you were the center of his universe. Today, he is a little man. He demands you leave him alone to accomplish tasks. He finds tasks of his own, some tasks to your dismay. Sometimes, accepting your new parental role can be terrible, too. Pun intended.

You can navigate the Terrible Twos with the least amount of turmoil by learning from the parents who have already survived.

Developmental Milestones

Every parent has a natural instinct which makes them look at other people's children and compare one to the other. By virtue of parenthood, every parent's heart is set on having the best, most perfect child. So how does your child compare to his peers?

Other parents can give you an idea of when your child will do things. A mom from daycare will tell you when your son will first try to fly like Superman, with a bath towel as a cape and off of the dresser. A dad at the playground will tell you when your daughter will first get in Mommy's purse and put on lipstick, and ink pen rouge. Share these funny stories about your own child with other parents.

Be careful not to compare physical and mental development of your child to another, as to do so can cause unnecessary anxiety. Each and every child matures differently. While some developmental milestones gauge gross motor skills, like walking, others gauge mental maturity, like identifying body parts and complex speech. Every child reaches each milestone in his own time. Some children walk at ten months, while others wait until fifteen months to take that first step. These differences are not cause for alarm.

Pediatricians can give you a clinical guideline of what your child should be doing at what age. Know the doctor's guideline is not a finite list. You should not panic if your child fails to meet a deadline. If your child fails to meet more than three, consult with a pediatrician about development. A pediatrician will refer you to a developmental pediatrician in the event of a suspected disability or delay.

The following guidelines are not set in stone. Since each child develops at his own pace, you will see your child months ahead on some tasks and equally behind in others.

16 months old

- Turns the pages of a book when you read
- Walks well, maybe backwards

- Sings
- Is upset when he gets frustrated
- Has chosen a favorite toy
- Starts climbing and exploring
- Says up to 10 words

17 months old

- Runs
- Favors certain games and toys
- Follows simple directions
- Says up to 15 words
- Uses certain words regularly
- Likes to ride toys

18 months old

- Runs well
- Says up to 20 words
- Feeds himself with a spoon
- Is picky about some foods
- Scribbles

19 months old

- Feeds himself with spoon and fork
- Says between 20 and 50 words
- Puts words together in pairs or small (3-4 word) sentences
- Brushes teeth with help
- Takes off clothes with help

20 months old

- Takes off clothes without help
- Knows when something is wrong
- Pretends to help pick up toys
- Imitates adults while playing (feeding a doll)
- Can learn up to five new words per day

21 months old

- Builds with blocks and toys
- Learns five or more words per day
- Walks up stairs with little assistance
- Walks down stairs with assistance
- Shows signs of bladder control

22 months old

- Imitates others' behavior
- Follows two-step directions
- Starts to learn up to ten words per day
- Shows good signs of bladder control
- Opens doors

23 months old

- Walks down stairs
- Identifies his own body parts
- Does inset puzzles
- Names pictures in familiar books
- Takes off clothes without assistance

24 months old

- Half of his speech is understandable
- Uses 40 words appropriately
- Makes three and four word sentences
- States likes and dislikes
- May start asking "Why?"

Now, officially begins the terrible twos. The milestones are no longer measured by the month. Again, though, your child may do some of these things long before his second birthday, and some others he may just hold off until after his third.

- Uses at least 50 words appropriately
- Follows two-step directions
- Masters physical activities like throwing, jumping, climbing, hopping, stacking and skipping

- Starts asking more questions, specifically more "Why" questions
- Likes being more independent: Dressing, brushing teeth, self-care
- Puts together sentences
- Attention span gets longer
- Becomes more social and seeks out others for play
- Shows interest in potty training
- Notices when routines change
- Shows interest in what motivates others to do things
- Starts to change speech pattern (words and tone) with audience (another child, a caregiver)
- Asks why people act certain ways (Why is Mommy happy?)
- Notices and shows interest in the anatomical differences between boys and girls
- May create an imaginary friend

If you are worried your child is not developing on pace with his peers, consult the Center for Disease Control (CDC) website for more information on child development and warning signs for developmental delays.

Talk to your pediatrician. Write a list of questions and concerns before you go to the doctor so you will be sure you have covered all points before you leave. If you are unsatisfied, see another pediatrician in a separate practice for a second opinion. You know your child far better than anyone else. Trust your instincts.

How Much Do Two-Year-Olds Understand?

Toddlers are individuals. In short, each one is different, yet they all have some similarities.

Once mobile, toddlers begin to develop a spatial sense which helps to protect them from objects in their environment. Their acute hearing begins to differentiate between tones of voices. They learn to control the volume of their own voices, seeking appropriate conversational responses. As toddlers begin to make choices, they encounter consequences. These consequences affect future choices.

Vocabulary blossoms, and sentences replace babbles. The dreaded "why" questions begin because they are learning cause and effect. Secondary and complex problem-solving skills emerge. Gross motor skills give way to fine motor skills. Talents form.

An awareness of independence awakens. Toddlers begin to show interest and excitement in the activities of others and try to join in the fun. They will appropriately exhibit displeasure, disappointment, happiness, anger, love and aversion. Likewise, they will identify these emotions in others. Empathy develops and with it comes compassion. A sense of right and wrong forms.

You are watching your child mature before your eyes.

Were You Talking To Me?

Terry is talking up a storm. The sentences are simple, but you clearly understand their meanings. Whether it is "I go bye-bye" or "I no brush teef", you get the picture. Just because he is not an orator, don't think for one second he does not understand.

Babies recognize their own names as early as four and a half months old. By a year, they know about 50 nouns. By 18 months, they are adding verbs and understanding how sentences work. During the next year, they experience a language explosion, learning up to 20 words per day.

At two, his vocal vocabulary may be four to five hundred words, but he understands around 1,000. His receptive language also includes the body cues we don't even notice we give away.

For instance, with your toddlers playing on the floor, you tell your coffee mate, "Terry yanked the cat's tail this morning. I don't know what to do with him!" Your child knows his name, "cat" and "don't". He also knows you are frustrated and angry by your tone, hand motions and facial expressions.

This is a two-way street. When you talk proudly to the neighbor about your child, he is going to pick up on your good vibes, too. Instead of talking as though he was not there, include him in the conversation to help build his linguistic and interactive skills. "Terry, tell Mrs. Kelvin about the puzzle you did this morning."

Take care when talking when your toddler is within earshot. Take even more care with negative things. Even without understanding them, toddlers can remember words and phrases. Later, when they learn the words, they discover the meanings of the phrases.

When toddlers continually hear statements like "Shelly's shy," or "Paul is a hitter," they decode these labels when they are older. Some children will take the label as part of their identities once they learn the meaning, making these descriptors self-fulfilling even when they are most appropriate as a stage rather than personality traits.

If you must talk about your toddler while he is in the room, keep the conversation upbeat and happy and include him. Save any worried or frustrated conversations for nap time or after bedtime, when the door between you and him can be closed for safe measure.

Monkey see -- Monkey do

"Imitation is the grandest form of flattery."

Your two-year-old loves you. She is going to mimic everything you do. And everything her big brother does. And everything the babysitter does. And everything anybody at your house does.

With her mastered mobility, she is going to try on your shoes in a number of new ways. She has been playing pat-a-cake and peek-a-boo. She has toddled along when you walk. She has copied the things you say (especially "NO"), but now she can do more.

When you talk to your friend over iced tea, watch her sit beside you and mimic your hand movements, out of the corner of your eye. When you apply make-up, watch her expressions in the mirror as she pretends to do the same. Has she pulled a chair up to the sink while you were washing dishes? These are just a few examples of mimicry.

Mimicry is one of the best teaching tools in your parenting toolbox. Wield it often and proficiently. When she mimics you, build her vocabulary by naming all the things involved. You've been to the grocery. Show her (and name so she can mimic) the bags, the cans, the cabinet, the shelf, door, knob, box, cereal, milk, bread, eggs, all the way to the receipt.

Beyond the vocabulary lesson, there is a bonding. You respect her enough to acknowledge her participation as valuable. This is the foundation of respect which will make her teen years tolerable without a straight jacket.

You are going to catch her mimicking other things as well. She may already be feeding her dolls with a spoon or reading to them at nap time. Has she brought you a bandage for your boo-boo? This is where parental fear of all things children do not fear comes to bear.

A two-year-old can mimic something she has seen only once. If you take her to the laundry room and show her taking clothes from the washer to the dryer. The next time she goes to the laundry, she will assume you will be putting clothes in the dryer, even if she has not been there in over a week.

Use your parental caution when doing chores or household duties around your toddler which you do not want her to mimic under any conditions...like hammering. This is also why poisons, such as cleaning supplies and drain solutions, must be kept out of little hands' reach. She sees you use it and cannot understand the danger in her using it as well.

Memory and Recall

Terry knows when you go to Grandma's house where the cookie jar is. He knows when Daddy goes out to the garden; cherry tomatoes are a sweet treat before dinner. When Johnny from next door comes over, Terry will go get his ball to play catch like they did last time Johnny came over, two weeks ago.

When you pull out his favorite book, he will correct you if you read the pages in the wrong order. He can even point to the pictures when you ask him to find certain objects or animals. He might even know his name on the nameplate in the front of the book.

On the way home, he notices familiar landmarks. He associates logos with places he has been, like the big mouse and the pizza place with the ball pit. He may even recognize Grandma's house.

Don't think the only things he remembers are objects and places. He remembers activities and routines, too. When Daddy has on shorts and grabs a bottle of water, Terry may just grab the basketball. If Mom puts her purse on her shoulder, look for up-reached arms accompanied with "I go bye-bye!"

By this age, Terry is firm in his bedtime routine. He knows what comes right after bath and brushing his teeth. Other routines are part of his repertoire. He may show you his terrible side if lunch is not followed promptly by his nap time strictly because you scheduled a doctor's appointment for him.

Not all of the things he recalls will be repeated over and over. Just like mimicry, some things he will remember only having seen or heard or experienced them once. Even though he does not have the ability to explain what he knows to you, he knows a lot about the way the world around him works, where things are and what they are called.

Mad Science

Regardless of the name you give it -- trial and error, experimenting, driving you crazy -- toddlers learn by experimenting. This active learning builds skills she will need in school and in life. These experiments are the seeds of both math and science, and the ingredients are found in her toy box or in your kitchen: divergent, convergent and heuristic toys.

Divergent toys are those which have more than one purpose. Balls, blocks and nesting cups are divergent toys. Bouncing a ball helps her strengthen hand-eye coordination and visual tracking. Throwing a ball builds gross and fine motor skills to handle the ball and to get the ball to travel far enough to reach the catcher. This exercise also engages critical thinking. She must assess what to do differently to be more accurate. Catching a ball combines all of the skills.

Blocks introduce concepts including texture, stability, balance, weight, matching, alternating and stacking. Nesting cups introduce a different side of spatial relationships than the ball will: which one fits inside the other or graduation. When moved to the sandbox, they show volume and density. She does not even know she is learning the basis of what will help her succeed in chemistry, geometry and physics.

Convergent toys serve only one purpose. Puzzles and musical toys are convergent toys. The purpose of the puzzle is to find the solution. It is a spatial relationship/problem solving exercise. Musical toys, like drums, are simply to stimulate her senses. Convergent toys serve specific purposes, but they should not make up the bulk of your toddler's toys.

Heuristic toys are everyday objects. Rather than store-bought toys, objects in your home make good toys for your child. Measuring cups and spoons, tins, boxes, maracas or rain sticks, a whisk, a toothbrush. Expose her to different textures and shapes, as long as nothing has small detachable parts she could choke on or swallow. Store the heuristic toys in a natural fiber basket to add another layer of interesting texture.

Heuristic play has been around as long as babies. Studies are now showing infants and toddlers who have a combination of heuristic playthings and commercial toys are scoring higher in school. These toys help build the imagination of your child. You will definitely see the rewards when she goes outside to play and brings you her first brew of "yard soup".

The Wheels Turning

The thought process in your child's head is simply off the chart. He is processing information at a dizzying rate. Cognition is how he processes information.

Terry has a concept of time. If an activity is complete, it happened yesterday...even if it happened last month. His birthday (three months away) is tomorrow. If you are doing it right this second, it is happening today. Give him about a year before he grasps the ideas of days and months; mornings, afternoons and nights; minutes and hours.

He understands the if/then principle. If I drink my milk, then I get to go outside. If I throw the toys on the floor, then I have to pick them up. You need to be using the words "if" and "then" when you give him situations. You will strengthen this principle and lay the foundation for both time appreciation and discipline.

The mad science is not lost on him either. His experiments have taught him some consequences.

- No matter how hard I try, the big cup will not fit in the little cup.
- I cannot fit two bowls of cereal in one bowl just because they are the same kind.
- I can only put 22 blocks in a tower before it falls down.

While he may not be able to count to 22, he knows how many blocks he can stack. You will notice he will not attempt to put more on the top.

After he attempts to combine the bowls or cereal (or cups of juice), help him clean up the mess. He recognizes the similarity of the substances. His volume perception will take a little longer to develop. He will only learn it by experimenting. Move this experiment to the bathtub or out into the yard.

The trial and error method is important. Learning from mistakes lasts longer than lessons learned through memorization, like mimicry.

If Terry is getting frustrated from trying to put the big cup inside the small cup for the sixth time, intervene. Show him the correct way, but hand him both cups separately. He needs to do it himself to fully learn the lesson.

The success of figuring it out (even with your help) builds his self-esteem and encourages him to try more complicated tasks. When he attempts something you do not think he can do, step back. He just may surprise you. He may not do it the way you would have done it, but he may do it without your help. Give him the chance.

Chapter 2

Fostering Communication

Parents take for granted their massive ability to communicate. When the toddler comes along, his particular brand of communication is a foreign language to parents. While he may repeat the same phrase three times, Dad will still be scratching his head doing a verbal version of charades. Traditionally, Mom is slightly more fluent in toddler, which is attributable to the transition from understanding baby language.

So, how do you help your little one move from babbling baby to conversant toddler? Should you consider sign language or a second language?

Linguistics

The first hurdle for any toddler is to learn to communicate effectively. If you have not kicked the pacifier yet, now is the time. Communication begins with the babbling of "ma-ma" and "da-da" and continues well into college. Next, your little one will be pointing or using her hands to make signs. She may even use a different "language" to speak to her siblings.

Many different avenues are available for travel to effective communication. By adding single words and phrases, gestures and facial expressions, soon your two-year-old will become a master communicator.

Two is the perfect age to add a second language. Whether the first language is sign language or the parent's native tongue, your two-year-old is ready to express himself in his first language, expand to a second language and can readily become fluent in both.

Itty, Bitty Sweetums

Parents are the first introduction children have to language. Toddlers love to mimic. Talking to your two-year-old is the first line of attack in expanding his vocabulary. Since he responds to you in a baby voice, you may be tempted to speak to him in baby talk. Resist.

It is far easier to teach him to speak properly than it is to un-teach him something you taught him. Rather than babbling to him, speak. Use real words, not nonsense or gibberish. Now, talking to him about quantum physics may be going a tad overboard, but having a normal conversation is not out of the question.

There is no shortage of subject matter. Think of yourself as the narrator in a movie. Narrate what you and your child do during the day. Whether it is the steps to making a peanut butter and jelly sandwich or how to get the correct mixture of sauce to spaghetti, talk about everything.

As cute as his "r" that sounds like a "w" is, do pronounce words correctly. Over time, he will learn to control his tongue better and produce the "r" sound. Those baby pronunciations will disappear. Use his acute mimicry skills to produce more and more words you can understand.

Test how much you understand by repeating what you think he said. If you get it right, he will let you know with either a big smile or more chatter. If you miss, he will repeat the word or phrase until you do. The parallel benefit of repetition is it validates you were listening to what he had to say. Everyone who speaks likes to know someone was actually listening to what was said.

Once you can understand, if he is still not pronouncing it correctly, others may not be able to understand. Continue to learn new words, but return to words he knows to perfect the pronunciation. The outside listener also needs to be able to understand him in your absence.

Remember, learning language is a cumulative exercise. Words build on one another.

Level With Him

Having someone talk down to you is degrading. Terry already knows he is smaller, physically and intellectually. Don't emphasize it more than absolutely necessary.

Get on his level.	Kneel down to talk to him or sit down. Look him in the eye when you have a question or when he does. Pick him up, and set him on your level. Making eye contact is a lesson you can only teach him by example.
Get on his level.	Intellectually, you are his superior. You have his entire teenager-hood to lecture him. Speak to him in terms he understands, and encourage dialogue. Use short sentences.
Listen.	You may not understand everything he is saying, but you will understand the most by actively listening to what he is saying. Repeat what he says to be sure you get it right.
Honesty is the best policy.	When he asks you something, respect him enough to tell him the truth in terms he will understand. If you don't know the answer, be big enough to admit it. Assure him you will help him find the answer to his question.
Respect him.	While he may well do or say something which will give your office mates chortles around the water cooler, do not burst out in guffaws in front of him. He will love to laugh with you, but will be offended if you are laughing at him. Trust is a tenuous thread you do not want to break now.
Enjoy.	This is truly a very short time in his life. The communication between you is open and honest, the way you want it to stay.

Sing, Play & Read

Reading to your two-year-old is one of the most important activities in your daily routine. If you did not read the last sentence, reading must be in your daily routine. Whether you employ the goodnight storybook or the afternoon rocker reading or the book over breakfast, read to your toddler everyday.

If you can, do all three. Just remember, Terry's attention span is not but about ten minutes unless he is very interested in the subject. Short books with short text per page and bright illustrations or photographs are best at his age. Board books are good for him to peruse on his own. Alphabet and beginning number books are filled with bright colors and familiar pictures. Now is the time for his first picture dictionary.

Once he picks a favorite book, read it regularly. When you read it, read the pages more independently from the text. Ask him about the pictures. Ask him what comes on the next page. Ask him to help you turn the page. Reading does not have to be a solitary exercise. While you are pointing at the words, he should be pointing at the pictures.

Nursery rhymes and songs are another way to get him talking. He is already using a sing-song cadence in his babbling to his toys as he mimics conversations he hears between you and your spouse and friends. Rhymes and songs both expand vocabulary by introducing rhyming words.

Singing helps him stretch vocal cords and produce different sounds than just talking. It helps him develop letter sounds more quickly. He will try and mimic the sounds he made while singing.

Playtime is a perfect time to talk. At the park, talk to him about the trees, squirrels, leaves, play equipment, grass, sand and everything else you see, touch or hear. Make sure you are having a conversation. Do let him get a word (or quite a few) in edgewise. He may not learn to say them all today, but he will file them away for another day.

Television is two-edged sword. Endless hours do not do your child good, as television talks to him instead of with him. Shows like *Sesame Street, Dora the Explorer* and *Blue's Clues* are geared toward encouraging language, based on their format. Small doses of this type show will help him learn. Use discretion when choosing programs for your toddler to watch.

Social Circles

Your two-year-old is the social butterfly with play dates and Moms-Day-Out and going to Grandma's house. When she comes home, she talks differently than when you dropped her off. You will notice more baby tones in what she says. She hasn't forgotten, but she has picked up on the speech of the other children.

Siblings will often use a different language to talk to one another when they are small, a language parents do not understand. During daycare, she is exposed to children who may not speak as well as she does and certainly do not speak as well as you do. Don't worry; she will not forget how to talk. You need to reinforce proper pronunciation when she does come home.

The quick tactic is to talk about her day on the ride home. Although she will not be the best one to answer in a Q&A session, asking questions fills her ears with words. You supplying answers to the questions you ask may get her to mimic the words she recognizes.

You may also be pleasantly surprised when she comes home having learned a new word. Celebrate new words with happy dances or high fives or the celebration of choice. Be certain she knows you noticed her new word.

And if it is not a word you would like to hear again, act like you did not hear it. Talk to the caregiver as to how she may have come in contact with that particular word.

Give Me A Sign.

Even if you did not start with sign language when your toddler was an infant, she started without you. She pointed at toys she wanted before she had words for them. She lifted her arms for you to pick her up. She put up her hands to mean stop.

You may be using informal signs with her without realizing it. Do you have a hand signal for "Come here"? Without learning all of the signs in American Sign Language (ASL) you can add signs to help your toddler communicate with you even before she knows the words.

The National Institutes of Health in Washington, DC has conducted long term research at the University of California on the effects of teaching infants and babies sign language. Research indicates signing actually speeds the learning of verbal speech and shows why it does.

Doctors Acreddo and Goodwyn, who conducted the research, found distinct advantages in groups of babies eleven to thirty-six months. Their study specifically examined the program "Baby Signs".

Expedited Speech Development

Babies who use sign language for attention get a parental response of many appropriate words which correlate to the signs. All studies to date prove that the more language a baby hears, the faster expressive language develops.

Reduced Frustration and Tantrums

By nine months, babies know both what they need and want. They get frustrated because they cannot use words parents understand. Without the advanced motor skills necessary to form words, they point, grunt and/or cry.

Parents are frustrated because they do not understand what babies want. Babies are frustrated because they cannot get parents to understand. Signing reduces these frustrations.

With signs like "thirsty", "hungry", "eat" and "cold" (and many other simple signs) babies can quietly, but effectively, let their needs and desires be known without tantrums or tears.

Increased Confidence and Better Self-Esteem

Looking at the core of self-esteem and confidence reveals how sign language is beneficial to babies. Self-esteem is the sense that one is perceived as praiseworthy and competent by one's self. Confidence is the same sense provided by those one loves.

Since signing provides effective communication to the caregiver, the caregiver's response is positive. Babies develop increased confidence and pride in their own abilities, which fosters better self-esteem.

Sign language allows babies to effectively communicate at a very young age and jump starts the neural substrate of verbal language. Speaking verbally requires planning, thinking and decision-making. These activities stimulate a baby's brain with lasting beneficial effects, including increased simple and complex problem-solving skills.

Parents use spoken language in concert with sign language. Just as parents associate the sound of the alarm clock with waking up, babies associate the sounds of parents' words with the sign for the word. The act of teaching the sign to the baby actually exposes the child to language at an earlier age. Both of these actions support the theory: Babies learning sign language hastens verbal language.

The benefits of infant sign language last into school years, expedite intellectual development and offer priceless bonding between parents and babies.

Bilingual

At two years old, your toddler is learning faster than she will at any other time during her life. She will learn more before she reaches her fourth birthday than she will from then until she graduates high school. If you want to introduce a second language, now is the perfect time to do it.

As with sign language, introducing a second language does not interfere with learning the native tongue. The advantages to learning a second language this early include native-sounding pronunciation (not influenced by the native tongue), lack of adult fear of making mistakes and the ability to process information in both languages.

Adults often encounter difficulty in foreign language conversation because they must translate what they hear to their native tongue before forming a response. Then, they must translate the response into the foreign language before speaking. Children originally taught two languages develop fluency in both.

Studies are revealing bilingual children possess superior language skills over monolingual children. In an effort to support bilingual children, more preschool television programs are featuring bilingual vocabulary, like *Dora the Explorer* and *Go, Diego, Go!*

Words already mastered in the native tongue should be the first words taught in the second language. Introduce new words in both languages simultaneously.

No, No, No, No, No, No, No

After hearing the word "no" and assessing its meaning, your two-year-old will use "no" more than 3,000 times before his third birthday: An average of ten times per day. What is so appealing about such a negative word?

Litany

Granted: No is easier to say than yes. Granted: He is going to say no even when he means yes. Granted: He is going to say no because he can.

- Do you want to go to Grandma's house? No.
- Do you want some ice cream? No.
- Do you want a kick in the shins? No.

All of these no answers are him exercising his new word. He has the mechanics of the word mastered, but does not yet have the meaning attached to the mechanics. He understands when you say *no*, but he still does not associate his *no* with the power of your *no*.

Authority

You have been exercising your authority with no.

- No, you cannot have cookies for breakfast.
- No, you cannot jump on the bed.
- No, you cannot draw on the dishwasher.

So, the first time Terry says, "NO!" he is doing precisely the same thing. He knows *no* means a boundary. He is setting his own boundaries. He will be telling you *no* when you try to get him to do things he would rather not do.

The litany of "No-No-No" will quickly become authoritative. *No* will begin to mean *no*.

- No. (Meaning: I do not want a nap.)
- No. (Meaning: I am not hungry for carrots.)
- No. (Meaning: I don't think a bath is a necessity.)

Choice

Terry has set some boundaries and is beginning to grasp the concept of questions and situations presenting choices. When he uses no inappropriately, engage him with questions where no is a viable answer, even though it may not be the answer he really wants.

It is lunch time, and you set his plate. When he uses no to mean "I am not hungry for carrots", ask him if he would like to go to bed. His answer will definitely be "NO!"

Be cheerful and happy! "Great! Eat your carrots." Even without the verbal skills to argue the point with you, he will absorb the lesson: "No" cannot be a pronoun for everything. Where he thought the first *no* would get him a sweet treat in place of carrots, his second *no* did not reinforce the first. Instead, it put the carrots right back on his plate and took away any chance of having them go anywhere except his mouth.

He also learned that *no* does not have a cumulative effect. It will take a few more years for this lesson to completely penetrate his consciousness, but subconsciously he will shift away from the litany of *no*.

Learning that *no* eliminates options is an important lesson for him. In fact, it will be the foundation of weighing consequences before his responses when he is older.

Very shortly after learning *no*, toddlers grasp the power of the little word. They find it creates boundaries, carries authority and eliminates choices. As the third birthday nears, *no* will be a less frequent occurrence than during the litany stage.

Are You Ignoring Me?

You know he heard you. Yet, he is going in the opposite direction. Your two-year-old is ignoring you. But, why? Why is my two-year-old ignoring me?

Two-year-olds are mastering their autonomy. Being assertive is an integral part of that autonomy. Be comforted by knowing they do it with the people they trust the most: You.

Impulse control is not yet fully formed. When you tell your child not to chase the cat, he is not going to be able to think about anything else. When you ask her to hand you the trash she just picked up, she is going to run away giggling.

What should I do when he ignores me?

Eventually, he will have to listen to you, and leave the cat alone. In the meantime, getting him to cooperate while giving him safe opportunities to develop autonomy is a balancing act.

Be realistic.

Be clear.

Keep it simple.

It's dinnertime. You say, "Get ready for dinner." What are you asking? Two-year-olds do not have enough experience to understand this vague concept. Instead try, "Wash your hands."

"Clean your room." This multi-step process is far beyond your child's understanding. "Put your books on the shelf," is a directive she understands.

Realistically, your child can handle one and two step directives. He cannot grasp abstract concepts and complex instructions which require three or more successive steps.

Follow through.

Are his hands still dirty? Walk him to the sink and wash his hands. Are her books on the floor? Take her to the books, and help her put them on the shelf.

Do not react to the ignoring by repeating the directive or having your own tantrum. This validates the behavior as one which gets attention. Don't ignore the ignoring. Make the child comply with your direction.

Motivate compliance.

Your child should abide your requests because it is the right thing to do. You don't want him to do as he is told because he is afraid to not comply. Remember, "because I said so" is not a valid reason to do anything.

Two-year-olds crave praise. Compliments are valid currency. "Thank you for being a good listener," and "Great job putting away your books so quickly," are statements which will motivate your child to want to do the right thing.

Incentives are great motivators. "When you put your shoes in the closet, we can look at a book." Notice the first word: *When*, not *if*. If gives the element of choice, which should not exist. He must put the shoes in the closet.

Stickers and charts are another good motivator. A sticker or stamp is rewarded when you only have to request once. If she collects five, she gets a special treat or an outing or a small toy.

Alternatives to "no"

"No. Don't chase the cat." "No. Don't throw the ball in the house." How many times a day are you saying *no*? Your child may be ignoring you because you say *no* too often.

"Let's sit down and play with the cat." You are still ending the chase, but not saying *no*. "Let's go outside to play ball." Now, you are demonstrating where ball should be played, instead of stifling what he wants to do.

When she is excited about something new, stay away from "No. You're too little." Encourage her by being excited with her. "That looks fun! I will help you." She may just surprise you by being successful. If she fails, encourage her to try again another time.

Some days you have to say *no*. Use it when there is no negotiating room: Running in the street or playing with Dad's autographed baseball. Choose your battles. Your child's environment should be safe and stimulating. Try a trip to the children's room of the arts and science center rather than the international tour of Ming vases.

Be understanding.

Some of your requests will be an interruption and unwelcome. Think about how you would feel if while sipping your tea reading this book, someone rushed in and demanded you get in the car. You would likely ignore the demand as well.

When you can, ease transition and give your child some warning tasks are changing. "We are leaving soon," is a good example.

You will not always have time to bargain with your child or the energy to beg them. Even with warning, he will not like having to abandon the blocks in favor of a trip to the market. Small transitions help smooth over the ruffled feathers.

When is it too much?

Trust your instincts. If you think your child is ignoring you more often than he is listening, talk to your pediatrician. A doctor may screen for hearing impairment or recommend a developmental or behavioral evaluation.

Chapter 3

Empowering Good Choices

Life is full of choices, even for toddlers. Good decision-making skills must be fostered early. Helping your child to choose and providing safe choices for him are how you can empower good choices. Good choices build self-confidence. Self-confidence leads to even better choices. This is a victorious circle, not a vicious one.

We all know to pick our battles. We know which we really need to fight and which ones really are not that important. You make these choices everyday. How do you win the battles worth fighting? Start by defining what victory means to you and Terry.

Victory comes in teaching your child to make the right choice. Whether sharing, meeting new friends, participating in play dates or visiting Grandma's house, toddlers can make good choices.

Choices are better than commands. This concept will take you far in your parenting journey. Choices are the doorway to trust and empowerment and the stone wall against rebellion. Learning the art of crafting choices can make the issuing of commands a rarity.

Easiest Way to Get Toddlers to Share

The time has come for your little one to learn she is not the only child in the world, despite her parent's belief she is the best child. Sharing is an action which comes easier to the empathetic child, and may never truly come to the obstinate or selfish child. The key to sharing is learning ownership and respecting boundaries. Sharing also offers parents the chance to teach children the concept of charity.

Ownership

To your two-year-old, everything she holds is hers. How many times have you heard the word *mine*? A bookie in Las Vegas would lay odds 10-7, as often as you have heard Mama. So how do you get her to understand ownership?

Identify all objects by their owner.

- Hand me Daddy's keys.
- Put away your doll.
- Where is Mommy's spoon?

Before she resorts to the toddler version of "possession is nine-tenths of the law", show her that ownership is in the object, not in the possession.

Sharing is not owning.

Showing her that sharing is temporary is the turning point to getting her to share willingly. Ask her if she would like to share your keys. Hand her the keys, and let her play with them. Gently take them back after a few minutes.

Next, ask her if you can share her doll. Cuddle and talk to her doll. When you return the doll, thank her for sharing her toy with you. She will understand the doll is still hers: You did not keep it; You returned it; and she still has it even though she handed it to you.

She will begin to recognize the word *share* as well as the fact that it is not a transference of ownership. Even before she can pronounce it, she will be able to perform it.

Borrowing is sharing.

Make a big deal every single time you use something belonging to someone else. Make an even bigger deal of returning it to the owner.

Ask your husband to share his pen for you to add an item to your grocery list. Thank him for sharing his pen with you. Have older siblings to exaggerate the sharing game as well.

Instead of borrowing your neighbor's drill, tell her how nice he is to share it with you. This shows sharing as something done outside the family as well and helps her to share in social situations like daycare or play group.

When she shares with you, be sure to praise what a big girl she is being to share her toys so nicely with you. By showing her adults and older children share regularly, she will take sharing as a normal part of the growing up process.

Patience is a virtue.

Some toddlers are not developmentally or emotionally ready to share. If sharing causes stress, do not force the issue.

Sometimes, toddlers fear their toys will be taken away and never returned. Other toddlers feel parents are showing favoritism to the child with whom the toy is shared. Although, as parents, we know these are both false, they are not unreasonable fears for a two-year-old.

Be patient. Continue to role model sharing and encouraging your child to share at home. In time, she will share. Sharing is a complex concept which will not be mastered in an afternoon. Over time, it will become a natural habit for your child. No matter how selfish she may seem today, she can become a sharing three-year-old. She may even surprise you and share long before her next birthday.

...But this is mine.

There are some things which parents should not ask their children to share. Blanky or a favorite stuffed animal holds a huge emotional investment for your toddler. These security objects are not good for teaching or enforcing sharing.

When other children will be at your home, put these items out of reach. When you go places where there will be other children with whom your child should share, leave these things at home or at least in the car.

Other parents will understand the precious, un-sharable nature of special toys, but other toddlers may not. Avoiding the stress is by far the best solution to this instance.

Caught You!

Just like making a big deal of sharing and returning objects, make an even bigger deal of independent sharing. As she gradually grasps the concept, she will share when you are not exactly paying attention. She will share with her dolls or stuffed animals. Praise the spontaneous sharing profusely!

She will also come to you with other opportunities to share. Whether it is an offer to share work by doing her tea dishes with the dinner dishes or a gift of one of your prize tulips while she keeps three, praise the fact she is sharing with you. She wants more than anything to please you and has already determined sharing is a great way to do it.

If she shares in a way you wish she would not, take it up with the other entity. For example, if she is sharing her broccoli with the dog, admonish the dog for begging at the table. She does not see the difference in sharing with the dog and sharing with her dolls.

In the case of your tulips, we will cover this scenario in Chapter Six "Discipline".

Charity begins at home.

Once your child is sharing, even the slightest bit, begin laying the foundation of giving. Giving is the logical extension of sharing. Start with very simple ways she can share and give.

It is snack time. Give her two cookies and say, "Daddy does not have a cookie. Give one cookie to Daddy." Daddy should profusely thank her for sharing cookies with him and join her in enjoying snack time. After a few repetitions of this exercise with Daddy or her siblings, she will surprise you if you only give her one cookie. She will tell you who does not have a cookie, even if it is you.

This simple exercise will help her to share toys, food and objects with others when she is in groups of her peers as she gets older.

Encouraging Toddlers to Make Friends

Now that your two-year-old is mobile and verbal, you have come to realize all of your conversations are about children's television programs and toys, sprinkled with the ever-present "Don't touch that," and "Give me that." The simplest solution is to introduce your toddler to his peers. Sounds simple, right?

What happens when you schedule the first play date and find out your child has no interest in his peers, is fearful of these little strangers or is a bully? You realize you will have to encourage your child to make friends. The discovery of other people began the moment your child was born, but so far, he has adults in his life. Those adults are rather predictable. They say and do things the same ways. In short: They are familiar. Now, you want him to withstand other children who are as volatile and unpredictable as he is.

Set An Example.

Everyone who is not a friend is a stranger. In order for your two-year-old to get comfortable with people outside his familial circle, he first needs to be exposed. When you take him out, are you saying hello to strangers who pass on the sidewalk? Do you make small talk with the cashier? Do you wave to the teller at the bank who gives him a lollipop? All of these things are the baby steps to friendship: They are icebreakers.

He does not have the experience to know how to strike up a conversation, but he does know how to wave. Smiles are contagious, and a child's smile will elicit an adult's full-face grin. Being friendly to others is a behavior your toddler will gladly mimic.

Introducing...

When introducing your toddler to a caregiver, an adult or another child, get on his level so you are seeing the new person from his perspective. This posture is comforting to your child because you are close and within reach if he feels insecure about this new person. He may need a few words of encouragement, or a hug, to engage a new friend.

He will look to you for how he should react. You should smile and encourage him to talk to this new friend. Without getting up, offer you hand to your new friend, and shake hands. While he may not understand what shaking hands is, the tactile nature of shaking hands creates a bond which aids in building a friendship.

Offer to stay close, but encourage him to go with his new friend. Without standing up, let him walk away. From his perspective, this lets him know you are on his side while he ventures into this new territory. Stand by your word. Stay close and intervene if he appears stressed by the novelty of the new relationship.

A Walk in the Park

The sandbox is where many a friendship begins. When you bring your toddler to the park where other children are at play, don't expect him to dive right in with abandon.

Scout a place where he is comfortable playing. Position yourself where you are close to him and available to talk to some of the parents. As he sees you engaging new friends at the park, he will mimic this behavior. When he approaches other children, join in the fun.

At two years old, he is not going to be announcing his name to the children on the jungle gym, but he may stroll over and commandeer a truck from another child. While not the introduction you may have envisioned for your first trip to the park, it is a perfect opportunity to employ some of the lessons from home.

Giving the other child his truck back, while telling Terry not to take other's toys, gives you a chance to meet the parents and find out the other child's name. Introduce Terry to this new playmate.

For the first few trips, keep them short. Fifteen minutes is more than plenty. Social interaction beyond family for two-year-olds is not priority and should be completely recreational for parent and child.

The Play Group

When you joined the play group, you were convinced it was for your child. By now, you have come to your senses and realized: The play group is for the socialization of the parents. If your child enjoys one or two activities at play group, stick with it...if he is making friends.

Enjoying the activities is the easy part in getting your toddler to enjoy play group. Getting him to make a friend and abandon the organized activities in favor of imaginative play is the difficult part.

Over the course of four play group sessions, has he made a connection with another child? If not, next time, you play with your child and whichever child is closest to him. Engage both children with building the largest castle possible with all of the blocks they can find.

By including another child in your play, you showed him exactly how easy making a friend can be. Do not be surprised if other children join in the activity as well. This is mimicry in its purest form.

On your next play group date, he will toddle immediately away from you to seek out his friend from last time. If other children joined in, they will gravitate toward the tandem. Single-handedly, you have changed the reason for play group from a social activity for parents to a social gathering for children.

The transformation will be complete when the children begin to abandon the organized activities in favor of pretend play and imaginative games filled with gibberish mixed with the occasional word you recognize.

The Benefits of Choices Rather Than Commands

As a parent, you cannot make all of the decisions for your child. To do so would render your child incapable of sustaining himself in later life. Learning the parental art of giving children choices will influence how your child makes life decisions in the future.

Ruling with an iron fist has never worked in the political, military or parenting arena. Instead of telling your child, "You will eat all of those peas," you are better asking, "Would you rather have peas or beets?" What is the difference? They are still going to eat peas.

Giving a child the choice lets them build self-esteem, teaches the consequences of bad choices and engenders trust.

It's a Matter of Trust.

Children understand when they get to choose, it is a form of trust. You trust their judgment enough to give them options. Two-year-olds cannot fully comprehend the concept of trust, but they look at parents with trust.

The parental edge: Craft the choices so that the child cannot make a bad decision, but can still make one that will not be as pleasant as the child would have hoped.

In the example, the child who hates peas chooses beets, only to discover that beets are not any better than peas. Next time he will choose peas, but, no matter which choice, he still ate a balanced meal.

Give Empowerment.

Children feel empowered by decision, having the power to say "no". This control over their lives extents the trust. Self-confidence is learned by being allowed to choose for oneself.

For instance, the child who picked beets finds out that beets are fantastic! No more peas for her. She is confident that in the future she will be able to make good decisions.

Quash Revolution.

Commanding a child to do (or not to do) anything will lead to resentment and rebellion. Parents of terrible twos attest to tantrum laden meals, shopping trips and family functions where they have forbidden typical toddler behavior. Countless parents of pregnant teens, delinquent children and adults who lack any initiative to be responsible for themselves will attest to their parenting failure by forbidding their children certain actions.

This goes all the way back to the story of Adam and Eve. The one thing they should not have touched, they did.

The only way to avoid this revolting behavior is to make good behavior the only choice.

Craft the Choice.

Think of the dozens of choices you make every day for your two-year-old. How many of those could you let her make? (Hint: Don't say, "None.") Let me help you with some examples:

- Would you like to wear blue shorts or red shorts?
- Do you want a grilled cheese or a peanut butter sandwich?
- Which book would you like for me to read to you?
- Is Mommy or Daddy going to tuck you into bed?
- Will you drink milk or juice with your snack?
- Which shoe first, right or left?
- Do you want to play cars before we shop or after?
- Would you like to color or go outside?
- Do you want to be it?

Not only do each of these questions allow your child to have a mite of control over his world, they each allow him some autonomy as well. In the same breath, you are controlling his atmosphere entirely. He cannot make a bad decision because you have crafted his choices to all be good ones.

By giving a child a command, you are in essence throwing down the gauntlet. You have given them a choice which has no benefit. Do as you say, or do the opposite. Generally, your command is safe, where the opposite is just that: opposite.

In the end, giving a child a choice is better than giving a command. The benefits of choice are self-confidence and trust. As the choices become more complex, the benefits increase proportionately. Good life choices make for happy lives, a benefit of incomparable value.

Chapter 4

Reducing Frustration

Being two years old is frustrating. Parents' frustration is caused by the same factors as the toddlers'. This time is filled with upheaval. The discovery of self is intriguing and fun for the toddler, but can be scary as well. Parents are frustrated by toddler's unsuccessful attempts far more than toddler is.

Independence is coveted, but brings growing pains to all involved. Natural parenting instincts impair the parent's ability to let go enough to let toddler find out consequences for himself.

Separation anxiety may surface as toddler takes his first steps away from home. Security becomes more than a blanket, and schedules now include activities away from home.

Start with your own frustrations, since they are amplified and adopted by your toddler. Once you have your frustration in check, Terry's will recede and disappear when you foster his budding independence and increased proficiency.

How to Foster Independence

Time has come for your little one to do some things all by himself. Some are little things: Holding the spoon, wrestling with a shirt to get it on backwards and wedging that right foot into a left shoe. How and when do parents present opportunities for toddler to venture out on his own?

Two is the age where your child is more interdependent than independent. He relies on your help, but is not totally dependent on you, like he was as a baby. Find the balance between doing everything for your child and making him do everything for himself. Listen to his cues, as he will let you know he is ready to try it solo. This timing is the key to fostering independence.

Explore

Just like when he was a baby and put everything in his "oral encyclopedia", your toddler wants to explore and experience everything around him. Encourage this behavior. Ensure his safety, but allow him to explore and try new things on his own or with your assistance (if he needs it). Exploration with the security of boundaries is the recipe for learning independence.

Use this time to talk to your toddler about the cause and effect principle. If he runs in the house, he could trip and hurt himself. Talk about all of the exploration. A dump truck and shovel with dirt in the back yard or baby doll and water in a tea set in the house...keep the words flowing.

Take some time to look at the world through your child's eyes, too. This time is short and enjoying it with your child is a big part of making it successful.

Endorse Autonomy

Do not assume he needs your help. Let him try. If he succeeds, applaud, high five, happy dance, cheer! If he does not, encourage him to try again, and this time, help him. Then, applaud, high five, happy dance, cheer! His blooming autonomy is his expanding independence. Show him you have faith in his abilities. That faith is the mortar between his talent blocks which build his self-esteem.

Allowing him to try some things alone which you aren't so sure he will accomplish is perfectly fine. Natural consequences are part of the learning process. Just like tripping is a part of learning to walk, he will learn to avoid hazards and keep himself safer. He knows you are there to help him and make it better if he does hurt himself.

Balance Expectations

While some experiments will meet with success the first attempt, others will not. Don't let that get you down. Expecting perfection from a two-year-old is a recipe for disaster. Your toddler wants to please you. If you set the bar too high for him to reach, he can feel your disappointment. This makes the building of self-esteem and autonomy impossible.

Play a supportive role and follow his lead. More often than not, he will be willing to try things you would not have thought him capable.

Congratulate his attempts, and celebrate his victories.

Increased Security

by Barbara Whitlock

(introduction by Ann Marie)

Your child is taking those first steps into the world without you ever-present. This can be as frightful for you as it is for your child. Your instincts call you to scoop her up and hug her tight. Realistically, your brain is nagging you to let go. She is getting to be a big girl and needs some space.

While you know what comes next, she does not. The big, wide unknown can make anyone insecure. But what do you do when she runs back to you and wants that hug? Scoop her up. When you put her down, know what you are going to do next: Make her feel secure enough to try it on her own.

How to Make Your Little One Feel More Secure

Baby's life began at his mother's breast, and remaining connected to mama forms his sense of security. Moving toward greater autonomy with secure separation becomes your goal as a parent.

Understanding a Toddler's Security Needs

Whether newborn, toddler or teen, every child needs to feel connected to his parent. How we stay connected to our children evolves over time. And how parents view that connection is quite different from how children see it. Time to put on toddler-sized glasses.

Parents -- and usually mom -- are like home base in a life-size game of tag. Children run along unknown paths, and sometimes in circles. They often feel chased, and may struggle, chasing something or someone. But "base" is the place where they feel safe; it's where no one and nothing can "get" them.

Mom is home base. She's the safe place, where you are protected, safe-guarded, nurtured, held close. She's your retreat from the world's challenges. She provides emotional bailout, or just remains that constant fixture you can dash back and touch -- like the large oak tree which serves as base in the backyard game of tag.

Security for a toddler comes from secure attachment. Attachment is a lifeline for a newborn, to ensure all his needs are met. That continues for toddlers. When your needs are met you develop trust. Trust in parents is the start-button for a psychologically whole life. It gives you the foundation that enables you to trust others.

Attachment Disorders

Not all children start off feeling loved and adequately cared for. Traumas can happen that wrest children from the comforts of their parents' arms. These can lead to attachment disorders. A host of problems follow from this loss of trust in primary caregivers: anxiety, depression, acting out, imploding within, social withdrawal, learning delays and psychiatric disorders.

It's not a pretty picture if a child starts life without secure attachment. Lack of trust haunts him for the rest of his life, though therapies can help. The attachment problems may be rooted in parental avoidance, ambivalence or inconsistent attachment. The net result remains a psychologically-damaged child.

But insecure children can also be clingy and demanding, striving to get attached and straining to find security and trust. Or, they may cut off or hold other people at a distance. In the worst instances, they turn inward and simply refuse to connect with others. These are symptoms of Reactive Attachment Disorder (RAD).

Traumas like a parent's death, abusive parenting or neglectful parenting can cause attachment disorders. But more subtle variables can also affect attachment: Parental mood shifts, emotionality, excessive transitions or even too many caregivers can strain attachment.

Clearly, home base -- the tree that becomes a mother's loving arms -- must be solid, whole, consistent and attentive to secure a child's primary attachment -- and ongoing connection. Consult professionals if you suspect attachment issues in your toddler.

From Healthy Attachment to Secure Separation

Healthy attachment is primary, and from this foundation children learn to separate naturally. But that doesn't mean separation will always be smooth, simple and seamless for every child.

Some children measure their distance to mother's lap meticulously. They won't go far, or they dash back frequently. That's fine when you're in the next room, but it's problematic if you get in a car and drive further away.

For most children, trial and error experiments assure them you'll return. While they worry at first, they grow more confident that you are just minutes away. Their comfort grows elastic, and you can stretch the distances and hours further. As you've always returned, they come to assume it. That's secure separation.

The Dos and Don'ts of Healthy Separation

Do   Spend loads of quantity (not just quality) time with your young children. The younger they are the more time you need to invest. Consistency is key to establishing and securing strong connection.

Do not   Pawn off your babies to others every chance you get. Make them primary in your life so they know you are home base.

Do   Hug them and give them attention when they ask for it. If they have a psychological need, meet it if you can. If you don't, that small need grows to frightening proportions.

Do not	Push away your children when they need you, in hopes that this will make them "tougher". This tells them you are not to be trusted; and they won't trust others either.
Do	Create separation opportunities as they get older, and introduce these gradually.
Do not	Show uncertainty, hesitation, or anxiety as you move away from them.
Do	Prepare your children for periods of separation, but use light-hearted, "no big deal" tones. Answer questions confidently and with reassurance.
Do not	Slip away without telling them, linger to enable clingy behavior or go back and forth for more than one goodbye.
Do	Smile, show confidence and move swiftly as you make your exit. Give them a quick hug and kiss and keep moving.
Do not	Hesitate, look back or show the least concern.
Do	Hug when you return, actively listen and affirm your child if they had a hard time with the separation. Tell them they'll handle this better next time, but use few words.
Do not	Show fear or guilt, or excessive concern for how your child expresses those feelings. Quickly redirect and turn the energy toward something positive.
Do	Keep moving gradually toward longer periods away, but start at small intervals.
Do not	Give up on your goal of helping your child separate securely from you. If your child seems to persist in not dealing well with these periods of separation, make them shorter and start at slower increments. But do not give up.

Start your toddler on a path toward secure attachment by devoting most of your time to him as a baby, and building that trust through meeting his needs and being ever-present.

As he grows, encourage his steps toward independence by celebrating his adventures from your lap and encouraging reasonable risk-taking.

Ensure his secure separation from you by using your acting skills to prepare and move confidently through brief periods of separation. Gradually increase these at intervals that seem appropriate for your toddler's needs.

Your toddler has you locked in his gaze. You're his home base, and he measures his distance to you at all times. Look him straight in the eye, act decisively and move in measured steps away from him as well. He'll learn you always come back.

Your toddler's security, like deep tree roots, will remain unshaken by the winds that blow you or him away at times. From that foundation he will bloom with the trust that produces a fruitful life.

How to Ease Separation Anxiety

That horrible day has arrived: The first day of school. Through the ages, it is well documented that the day is far harder on parents than on children.

Has your little princess just thrown herself into your arms, sobbing she can't go to school? You may have gotten a whiff of separation anxiety. If this is the first time she will be somewhere where you are not, it is separation anxiety.

Begin by being the adult. Show a stiff upper lip, encourage, ensure and be cheerful, even if you are crying on the inside. Then, leave. Separation anxiety has to run its course. You have avenues to make the trip shorter.

Whose is it?

The reality of most separation anxiety is: Parents have it, and they give it to their children. What?!

Children are not born with an innate fear of anything. As toddlers, they explore e-v-e-r-y-t-h-i-n-g. Why would going someplace new be a cause for fear? Logically, it is not.

Toddlers absorb environment, and their budding emotions are tied inextricably to their parents' feelings. You have already seen it:

> Daddy comes home from a stressful meeting and slumps in his chair. Terry comes over with furrowed brow and perches in his lap tentatively. He does not know what to do, but knows that proximity always makes him feel more secure. He is trying in his own little way to comfort Daddy.

So, in the opening scenario, who does not want to go to the first day of school, Princess or Mom? Chances are Mom is the one with the trepidation. Don't beat yourself up for this. Change is hard. Work on making it easier for yourself, so it does not even register on her radar screen.

It's no big deal

Now, you know it is yours. But what is it really? Look at the checklist and choose as many as apply:

○ **Buddies**   For the last two years, you and your child have been constant companions. Although you realize she is not your best friend, she has been a major component to your day which will not be there now.

○ **Schedule**   You scheduled everything around your toddler's naptime, meals and play habits. Your schedule has a gaping hole you are not sure how to fill.

○ **Unknown**   You knew the routine and everything which would happen next. You could always intervene to ensure nothing "happened to" Terry. Now, you don't know, and you are not there.

This is a fear.

○ **Control**   You controlled every situation for the optimum outcome: best learning toys, best foods, best playmates.

This is a fear.

○ **Worry**   You have always worried about the things she could get into at home, but now you are not there to protect her from the unknown things she could get into in her new environment.

This is a fear.

The first two are very easy to overcome. Overcome them before the first day your toddler goes to day care by changing your schedule and making plans to telephone or visit your friends and family. Do projects you have left neglected. Take up or return to a hobby. Read a book. Go for a walk. Shop alone. Get a pedicure or a massage. Take a nap. Fill the bathtub with bubbles and have a glass of grape juice (9:00 a.m. is really too early for wine).

Over the next weeks, you will rediscover all the things you did before the baby came along, and you will find new events to fill the time which involve your little one as well.

Fear is another animal altogether. It is the root of anxiety. Grab it by the horns and give it a firm shake.

Unknown

Go to the daycare. Spend a day, or three. See all of the activities your child will enjoy. Observe the way the caregivers interact with the children and one another. If you cannot stay all day, go on different days at different times to see how the day will progress for your child.

Ask questions of everyone.

- Where will you keep my child's clothes and diaper bag?
- Can I see the kitchen?
- Where is your Department of Health certificate?
- How many children are enrolled total?
- Do you have any children of your own?
- What do you use to clean the toys?
- Who has been trained in CPR?

If you think of a question, let it out.

The only way to abate the fear of the unknown is to know.

The only way to know is to see it for yourself or ask someone who does know.

Control

You are still in control. You chose the daycare. You went and investigated every lock on every cabinet. You know how many children everyone has and where their parents live. Relax. While always easier said than done, relax is precisely what you need to do.

Remember the day you introduced him to his best friend at the park? For the first time, he walked away from you and went into the big world to explore with someone his own size. Today is not much different. He is hand-in-hand with someone who is going to take care of him. His best friend at the park could not take care of him, but his caregiver can. This is an even safer situation. The adults are in the same room with the children or in a much smaller fenced area than a park.

If you feel the need to call the daycare on an hourly basis, you are on the borderline of being a helicopter parent. You are inhibiting your caregiver. If the caregiver is on the telephone with you, who is watching Terry? Let the daycare do what you are paying it to do.

Your child needs some time to socialize with others on his own. This is his chance to flex those sharing and friend-making muscles you helped him build. You will see him in a few hours, and he will be more than happy to babble all about it to you on the ride home.

Worry

Parents worry. It is part of the job description. There comes a time when worry is unhealthy. If you have taken the steps to cure the unknown and are still worried, you need to sit down with another adult and rationally discuss the worry.

If you have chosen caregivers wisely, investigated the setting and your child shows no ill effects from being in another's care, your worry may not have a basis. Talk to your spouse or parent or best friend about your fear. If the fear remains after that discussion, speak to a professional. This type of fear and anxiety is not healthy for you or your child.

Get Rid of It

If you have a handle on your separation anxiety, your child's should disappear simultaneously. On the off chance it does not, take concrete steps to make it disappear.

You may not need all of the steps. They can be used in any order according to what is most comforting for Terry. You may need to use two or three together. Mix and match to find what is best for your toddler.

1. **Talk about it as exciting.** "You are so lucky! You are going to go play at school!" Make it sound like an adventure. Talk about what will happen during the day and point out similarities to how things happen at home.

2. **Schedule.** If the daycare schedule is very different from your home schedule, adjust yours closer to the daycare. This will ease the adjustment for your child. Add in some daycare activities into your own schedule for two weeks prior to help your toddler ease into group activities.

3. **When you drop your child off, say goodbye, and leave.** Caregivers are trained to take your child and immediately immerse them in an activity. This distraction will give you time to make your exit. If Terry is going to fuss about your exit, it will not last long before he is engaged in a fun activity.

4. **Come back.** While this may seem like a no-brainer to you, remember your toddler understands more than he can speak. If you say, "I will be back right after lunch," as soon as he has a happy plate, he will be looking for you. Do not let him down. Come back when you say you will come back.

5. **Bring a surrogate.** If Terry has a favorite blanky or toy, buy a surrogate for daycare. Before you send it to daycare, wash it in your normal detergent. It will have a familiar smell and be a comfort to your child at naptime. If you snuggle it, it can even smell like your eau de toilet.

6. **Together time.** When you come back from vacation, the first thing you do is have a meeting to get caught up. For your toddler, a day away from you is equal to a week's vacation. Take time to have a briefing to hear about what he did, let him show you his work. Actively listen and comment.

7. **Congratulate.** Hugs and kisses for being such a big boy are in order. He went to "big boy school" and did all this fantastic stuff! Let him know how much you love him and how proud you are of him.

Separation anxiety should be very short-lived. Once you've overcome yours, your child's should not last more than two weeks. Call the caregiver a few hours after you drop him off to ensure the anxiety disappears.

If separation anxiety persists, talk to the caregiver and your pediatrician to isolate other possible causes.

The Benefits of the Schedule

Children feel safest when they know what to expect. They have a sense of control over their own world. Tantrums are often a result of interruption, whether of a nap, a mealtime or another scheduled activity. Your child is expressing her displeasure at events unfolding differently than she had planned.

Consider the safety net created by your own schedule. You need not spend time worrying or planning events which happen each day at the same time. Your morning routine is a prime example. Wake up. Attend to the restroom. Make the bed. Brew coffee. Fix breakfast. Pour the coffee. Sit down and enjoy the morning meal with the news. This schedule safety net provides a calm transition from sleep to the day. You perform it each morning with no extra effort on your part.

The schedule safety net gives toddlers room to grow and develop personality traits and define their character. Knowing how different children benefit from schedules is the key to developing the perfect schedule for your two-year-old.

Which kind do you have?

We all know toddlers are individual, but they fall into three large categories: sticklers, clowns and investigators. And yes, they all show some traits of each category.

Sticklers

This toddler is a stickler for details. He likes order and punctuality. His toys are arranged in an order he understands, and he enjoys sorting games. The schedule gives him a large sense of security.

Clowns

Often dubbed the "social butterfly", this toddler will be in the middle of the action with his family, peers and the pets. He loves fun in all forms. Schedules are a bit of a bother, as they represent an interruption to his merrymaking.

Investigators

He can take anything apart, be in three rooms at once and find anything you never meant for him to touch. He has two speeds: run and sleep. While you may think the schedule is really to regain your strength and sanity, it is just as much for keeping your investigator healthy.

What's on tap?

All toddlers need some basic building blocks in their schedules: meals, nap, play, bedtime ritual. The most important part of the schedule is sticking to it...no matter where you are.

Meals

Breakfast is a must. Whether you choose to make it in pajamas or after you get dressed for the day is up to you and your laundry capacity. Lunch and supper should be at the same time everyday. Snacks may be more flexible, but should not be skipped.

Your stickler might like a toy or paper plate clock to show what time meals are. This will reinforce his sense of order. Your clown may like to make meal times more of a game. Just because he has to do it does not mean it cannot be fun. Your investigator needs to be enlisted to help you make meals. Keeping his hands busy keeps his feet still.

Play

Play is how your toddler learns, so that makes it an important element to everyday. Changing what you play by day or week will help you isolate and strengthen certain skills in him, but playing at the same time everyday is important to his learning process as well. Remember, his sense of time is still "yesterday, today and tomorrow".

As routines settle, your toddler will anticipate activities. If he is awaiting a craft project with you and you go to the grocery instead, you have upset the balance in his world.

When the grocery shopping will not wait, cutting playtime short is an option, but omitting it is not.

A stickler may like playtime to be orderly, a game or building blocks. A clown may prefer play group or a neighbor coming to a tea party. An investigator may well be interested in digging bulbs in the flower bed or a game of tag.

Choose play activities which deplete your toddler natural store of energy both in the morning and the afternoon. This calorie burn will help manage mealtimes and sleep schedules more naturally than just with a clock.

Nap

The importance of a nap for toddlers cannot be understated. Toddlers need 10-12 hours of sleep everyday. They are not likely to get more than nine or ten overnight; therefore, a nap is a necessity. If you are going to avoid a terrible meltdown, you know a nap after lunch is imperative.

While the bedtime ritual is a well-known, oft-touted phenomenon, the nap ritual is not. Nap tends to be a variable in the schedule. If you have a lunch date with a friend or if morning errands run long, nap may begin in the car on the way home. This is where quality of sleep comes into play.

Transferring a sleeping toddler from a car seat to a bed may be easy or impossible, depending on which parent you ask. If the toddler could tell you, the answer would be *irritating*. Toddlers need two uninterrupted hours of sleep in the afternoon (or 5-6 hours after they awaken). Despite your cognizance of his awakening during transfer, you are interrupting his sleep.

You have to be the one to show discipline when it comes to the nap schedule. It must begin at the same time everyday. Don't be a bit surprised when your toddler resists going to sleep when the time comes. Over time, sleep will come.

Make the routine conducive to sleep. Turn off noise makers in the house. Darken the room. Take off shoes and restrictive clothing. Snuggle bedtime toys. Read a story. Kiss "goodnight". With few distractions, your toddler will doze off. If you don't find success in short order, increase physical activity in the morning and make lunch a little heavier. Everyone sleeps better on a full stomach.

Bedtime Ritual

It really starts before supper. Pick up toys before it is time to eat. This habit building will last a long time, or even a lifetime, if it becomes ritual as a toddler.

Time to wash hands and face. Your stickler may enjoy helping set the table. Your clown may like entertaining you while you finish cooking. Your investigator may find excitement in tossing salad. This is important bonding time, as meals are a family affair.

Eat and clear the dishes. Toddlers love to help. Let them. This is the last running around time. Praise whatever help you get, but don't be overcritical if you only get one spoon from the table after thirty laps around it.

Time for the toothbrush. Clean choppers are a necessity. At this age, let him brush first. Then, ask him if you can take a look. When you find something behind his teeth, you can make a pass over all of them to be sure they all got brushed. Letting him do it first will lead to him doing it correctly on his own sooner.

Next stop: bathtub. The bathtub is a magical place. It lends itself to many make-believe play sessions. It also is the spin cycle for the day. Just like laps in the pool make your tongue hang out, the bathtub can help wash the last of the charge out of your toddler's battery. Use this to your advantage.

Wash his hair when you first put him in the tub. While he plays, it will begin to dry. Staying in the tub is not going to do more than wrinkle his little toes, which makes for interesting conversation and great sensory input. Take your time in the bathtub. Invest in some tub toys which inspire imagination. Add some natural sponges and a loofah for textural input.

Use scrubbing time to name body parts, identify tickle spots and increase vocabulary. Naming everything helps him learn more words. Like you did with the toothbrush, let him clean first. You can always follow up if he misses that large dirty spot on his shin and the ketchup on his chin. Name everything all over again when you towel him off. This is brain exercise. If the potty is in order, now is the time.

Pajama time. Your investigator and your clown will want this to be a rambunctious time, but it needs to be a powering down time. Try a lullaby or a nursery rhyme while you get into pajamas to soothe the time. Resist all urges for tickling, as the raucous laughter works as a stimulant.

Story time. If your stickler likes the same book every night, consider that a victory. Investigators and clowns will not be so inclined. For them, choose a group of four or five quiet stories to cycle through during the week. Bedtime is not the time for stories which encourage giggles and tickles and funny faces.

Snuggle time. Whether it is night prayers or a lullaby or both, snuggle your little one. Kisses and hugs help him feel secure and loved. Say, "Goodnight," and leave the room.

But we're not home...

Keep as much of the schedule intact as possible. Without fail, keep the sleep portions of the schedule on time. Toddlers do not understand the concept of the weekend, nor do they understand you are on vacation when you visit your in-laws.

To keep your toddler's behavior out of the terrible end of the scale, keep him secure with familiar activities at familiar times as often as you can. The foods offered may be different, but offer them at the same time. The bed may be unfamiliar, but the nap and bedtime rituals will not be.

Exposing your toddler to a new environment is a genuine learning experience for him. He will absorb the new elements best if he feels the security of a schedule. His schedule represents what he knows. Everyone is more comfortable when they know what comes next.

Chapter 5

Managing Defiance

Toddler defiance is as much a fact of life as teen angst. Managing defiance as a parent through this stage need not be difficult! As the adult, you get to choose the battles without your toddler being any the wiser. Defiance gives parents an opportunity to empower independence and good decision-making in their toddlers.

By setting and sticking to limits, you are producing a safer and more stable environment for your toddler. Discipline becomes a way of life for the two-year-old. Boundaries for behavior are delineated.

Include schedules in your limits. Remember to schedule fun in your day as well. Reinforcing good behavior in greater measure to admonishing bad behavior fosters good behavior to the majority. "Thank you for putting away your books," or "It was nice of you to share your cookies," are gold stars toddlers love to collect.

Providing sleep and food in adequate measure, you can avoid the tantrums which spring from hunger and sleep deprivation. Try and employ a few techniques to build a good eating and sleeping schedule.

Defuse defiance by avoiding some of the defiant hot buttons. Choose appropriate times to run errands: Specifically, not during nap time. If the high chair in the restaurant demands a tantrum, get the food to go and have a picnic instead. As the adult, you not only control what battles are fought, but which ones are not. Your choice increases your success ratio.

Tips for Managing Defiance

While these techniques will not produce a completely patient preschooler in a matter of days, with consistent application, defiance can be reduced as your toddler learns that defiant behavior is not how to get her way.

The Big Picture

So, your fashionista wishes to wear her pink striped shirt with her orange and green flowered skirt...does it really matter? As long as she is warm, go with it. Color coordination takes a few years to develop.

Your budding chef wants chicken fingers for breakfast and pancakes for dinner. You are serving balanced meals; does it matter what order in which they are served?

Your future interior decorator thinks dolls should be lined up under the bed instead of on the bookshelf, and books should be in the toy box. With no tripping hazards on the floor, celebrate! Her room is clean, and she did it!

These examples are your toddler showing autonomy and individuality. Is it the way you would have done it? Not a chance. Is it worth seeing the terrible side? Again, not a chance.

Empower Independence

Today, you need to go to the doctor. Rather than have a fight over her despising your choice of clothes, let her decide whether she would rather wear the skirt or the pants that match her pretty shirt. Ask the chef if he would like peas or green beans with his breakfast!

Instead of just pointing out what cannot be done, give your toddler choices. It is just as easy to say, "Let's go outside and play ball", as it is to say, "Don't throw your baseball in the house." When she wants a cookie appetizer, let her decide between a piece of cheese and fruit slices.

To foster independence, you must give your child the power to make decisions about his world. You have the power to control which decisions he can make and the responsibility to limit his choices to ones which will be good for him.

Decision-making is the core of free will, the axis of right and wrong and the penultimate display of independence. Fewer choices (Limit choices to two.) translate to fewer frustrations and less defiance. The celebration of good choices fosters self-worth and self-reliance.

Time Out is Not Punishment

Let your child help design a chill out zone for time out. A big pillow, a few books, a cuddly animal: the makings of a great place to calm down. Call a "chill out" instead of the "go to your room" you got as a child. If he won't go, set an example -- you go chill out. This will reinforce that calming down is not a punishment.

By now, you know the signs which lead to a tantrum before it arrives. When defiance is going to rear its ugly head, scoop her up and sit on the couch...or better yet, Daddy's chair. A little snuggle time can combat the defiance.

Redirecting negative energy into a loving environment or a playful quiet time before it reaches the tantrum stage is a great opportunity to explore emotions with your toddler. Talk about happy faces and smiles and things you both enjoy. Defuse the frustration.

Distraction & Diversion

By avoiding some of the defiant hot buttons, defuse the defiance.

Plan shopping trips to avoid nap times. Sticking to your child's nap schedule is important for her growth and your sanity. Skip stores that will over-stimulate her. If the toy store does it, show her the carousel or the fountains. Better still, save the toy store for a day she is at Grandma's house.

Schedule doctor visits for the mid-morning or very late afternoon, especially on immunization days. The pain reliever before the appointment and the outing will make her tired and cross. She will be glad to be home and go directly to bed.

Respect Goes a Long Way.

When asking your toddler to do something, make sure he knows how. By picking up his toys with him until he has it down pat, you will not have the defiance related to frustration. Sometimes, responsibility can be overwhelming. When he feels like he is failing, he will be terrible.

Be reasonable in your expectations. He wants to please you as much as you want him to succeed. If it is not quite right, do not redo it for him. Accept his version. It is good enough. It is not how you would have done it, but you did not do it -- he did. Thank him for doing it.

Appreciate that your two-year-old has a unique concept of time. When you ask him to leave his fun play at daycare to get in the car, let him have a chance to switch gears. "We are leaving in three minutes," lets him know that time is short. Telling him again in two minutes reinforces the urgency.

With repetition, he will pick up on your routine and learn the second time you tell him, you will be getting in the car and going somewhere else, regardless of whether or not he melts down. You have taken the time to teach him a transition from something he likes doing to something he might not care to do without being terrible.

Why Toddlers Bite

"Toddlers biting is not that unusual." ~Anonymous pediatrician

There is little comfort in knowing that most children bite at one time or the other. So why do they bite?

Psychologists agree most children have bitten someone at least once or been on the receiving end of a bite. Fear, anger and frustration top the list of reasons why children bite. Someone having bitten the child is the next reason.

Major changes in children's environment can cause emotional upset which a toddler does not have sufficient verbal communication skills to express. This frustration, born of anger or fear, manifests in aggression.

Children also bite to gauge the reaction they will receive or to exert control over a situation. In which group does your junior vampire belong?

Investigate the nature of the circumstances in which the child bit to determine why he is biting. New baby, new home and/or new school are often the triggers for aggressive behavior. Toddlers do not have the understanding of their feelings and the words to say, "I do not like this."

This particular investigation should include all areas where the child is involved, including play groups, daycare and babysitting situations. Identifying the source of the behavior is necessary to stopping it from recurring.

Some children will bite to show that they are excited or over-stimulated. They choose biting to change the focus of the activity.

The bite effectively changes the focus from the current activity to the toddler's immediate need for attention. Time to calm the child is in order. Time out or a nap work equally as well.

Other toddlers will bite as a misguided attempt at affection. When the little vampire sinks his fangs into your shoulder, before you snap, gauge his reaction to what he has done. If your child appears to be proud of the "love nip", chances are that he has mistaken biting for kissing.

Gently showing him the difference will make the distinction more clearly to him. Do this by kissing, not biting.

Does she have a quizzical look? She may be trying to see what effect biting has on you. The best reaction is to cloud up as if to cry and explain that biting hurts. She may have seen this behavior elsewhere, or been bitten herself.

Make sure that she will be welcomed at daycare, play school or preschool by checking with the caregiver. She may be gauging her playmates' reactions to this new attention-getting technique she has discovered.

The most important thing to keep in mind is that children have no instinct to attack one another. Children's primary focus is to explore, learn and play with their friends, family and siblings. Once you pinpoint the reason behind the biting, curbing it is really simple.

Tips for Managing Hair Pulling

Some children begin hair pulling the moment they can reach a handful, whether Mom's, sister's or the dog's. Two predominant schools of thought emerge as to how to stop this behavior:

1. Pull the child's hair.
2. Don't pull the child's hair.

While the first would seem to show the consequences of hair pulling, to a two-year-old, it does not. Toddlers do not have enough experience to associate the pain of an adult pulling their hair and the pain they inflict on others. While understanding the cause and effect of "if you pull my hair, it hurts", they do not have empathy to understand it hurts someone else when they pull hair.

If one does not work, why does two?

Pulling hair is one of the ways that a toddler expresses himself and shows control over his environment. The three main reasons for hair pulling are:

1. He discovers that this behavior gets an instant reaction and wants to repeat the process. **Example:** I pull Sissy's hair, and she screams!
2. He tries to get adverse situations to change. **Example:** Sissy takes my toy. I pull her hair, and she drops it!
3. He is developing cognitive thinking to change the outcome of a situation. **Example:** Sissy has the last candy. I pull her hair, and she screams. She will either drop the candy or not take the last one next time.

So how do you stop this behavior?

Be firm. Be consistent. Stand your ground.

- **Show him it will not work.** If he pulled hair to get what he wants, take away what he wants and return it whomever had it. Tell him, "We do not pull hair. It hurts." Do this as soon as the hair pulling happens.

- **Interrupt the behavior.** When you catch him, untangle his fingers and tell him, "We do not pull hair. It hurts." Immediately impose a time out of a minute where he gets no interaction.
- **Talk it out.** After time out, ask him if he knows why the time out was imposed. When you know that he is associating hair pulling with time out, let him know that the most important point is: "We do not pull hair. It hurts."

Common mistakes:

This behavior will not go away on its own. The number one reason it persists is because hair pulling is effective. It either produces results or shifts the focus of the current social setting. You must intervene.

- **Ignoring the behavior.** When you ignore hair pulling, he learns that pulling hair gets him what he wants from the person whose hair is being pulled. This will encourage the behavior.
- **Distracting him from the behavior.** If you distract him with a book or a snack, he will not understand the social interaction of the situation. His interpretation is: *If I pull hair, I get special time.* Hair pulling becomes a positive experience.
- **Pulling his hair.** Toddler lacks the empathetic skills necessary to understand this is you showing him the result of his actions. Instead, he comprehends that pulling hair is going to change something, thus reinforcing his behavior.

Instead, model the behavior you want from him. Talk to him. You want him to talk to you (and others) when he wants something to change, rather than turning to physical means to get what he wants.

This is not a miracle cure for hair pulling. Two-year-olds need consistent reinforcement that this behavior will get the same reaction from you every time. Make a point to use the same words every time you talk to him about it. All caregivers should use the same words, so he does not think it only applies with Mom.

This technique is also effective for stopping such behaviors as kicking, biting, hitting and pinching. For kicking, hitting and pinching, introducing the idea of "nice hands and feet" will help get Terry ready for pre-school and kindergarten. Learning to keep his hands to himself and his feet on the floor is a big step toward learning how to behave and respect boundaries in school.

As his verbal skills become more developed, discuss the more appropriate behaviors of saying "No" or "I want to have that, please." Let him know this will be more effective and well-received than hair pulling.

Tips for Managing Tantrums in Public

Tantrums are a child's number one, guaranteed, attention-seeking behavior. Do not allow this fact to resign you to a parenthood filled with screaming and flailing. You can control your child's behavior as easily in public as at home; sometimes more easily.

Time-tested techniques are the best way in combating public tantrums. These are the secrets of those parents whose toddlers shop successfully, attend social functions without incident and epitomize "little ladies and gentlemen".

Whether you have friends in your home for a function or you are in a store, these seven simple steps will help you manage those screaming outbursts in public.

1. Do not be embarrassed by his poor behavior.

Being embarrassed will reinforce that his attention seeking method is valuable and effective. He has just become the center of attention as you become the shrinking violet into the draperies. Stand up and take the microphone firmly away from him. Remove him from the spotlight.

2. Be firm.

State that the behavior will not be tolerated. Let the child understand that she is not permitted to do this at home, and thereby will also be prohibited from this behavior in public.

Your tone of voice in this situation should not be angry, but should be firm and even. This is not open for discussion. You are "laying down the law".

3. Be consistent.

If this behavior warrants a time out at home, take time out now. A trip to another room, a restroom or in/outdoors can suffice. A silent period of reflection and stillness need not last long in public.

If you are not in a position to do it now, administer a time out as soon as you get home. Let him know right now the punishment will fit the crime and will not be bypassed strictly because you are in public.

4. Be fair.

If one child misbehaves, be sure to punish one child. When other children are present, one child may act out to seek attention. Taking everyone home from the playground 30 minutes before schedule is not fair to the other children. The one acting out should have a seat and think about why she is not getting to fully enjoy your outing.

Remember, time is relative. Two minutes of inactivity to a two-year-old is an eternity. Be prompt in ending time out and discussing the problem.

5. Talk about it.

The child who is punished will repeat the behavior if he does not understand the punishment is a direct consequence of his actions. After time out, be certain he understands how the chain of events was linked. Ask if he knows why he was punished. If you have to remind him, have him repeat it to you.

Explain to him that you are trying to make him a person who does not ever need to be punished. This reinforces you are not a monster punishing machine, but a parent.

6. Do not assassinate her character.

Telling a child she is bad is not healthy. Talk about the behavior being bad and unacceptable. "Taking the toy away from your brother is not the nice way to play."

Give the child examples of good behavior and explain that good behavior is expected. "When you want brother's toy, you have to ask him to please give you the toy."

Show the benefits of good behavior without bribing her into doing the right thing. "When ask for the toy nicely, we all get to play with the toys."

7. Be the adult.

You need not be a bully or condescending in order to discipline children in public. You need only be adult, consistent and understanding.

You can control your child's behavior as easily in public as at home, as long as the child knows that the rules are the rules no matter where you go.

Chapter 6

Discipline

Discipline is a controversial subject for most parents. Merriam Webster is partly to blame for the rift. Webster defines discipline first as punishment. While that is an accurate definition, in the parenting arena it is neither the primary nor a fully operating definition.

The obsolete definition of instruction has been effectively replaced and expanded to include the parental definitions of discipline:

- Training that corrects, molds, or perfects the mental faculties or moral character
- Control gained by enforcing obedience or order
- Orderly or prescribed conduct or pattern of behavior
- A rule or system of rules governing conduct or activity

Discipline strategy is the more common term used for discipline, in its behavior control definition. In terms of toddlers, parents need a strategy. Both successful and unsuccessful parents attest to the need for a system in advance of children. In short: You need a game plan. Punishment alone will not suffice as a discipline strategy.

Toddlers are named such because they do not have the knowledge and ability to walk without toddling or stumbling. They are not adept at self-control of their behavior, either. Parents need to be ready to catch toddlers when they fall, physically and behaviorally.

The discipline strategies which are most effective are those combining teaching, encouraging, reinforcement, consistency and, when necessary, punishment. Teaching good behavior is far simpler than correcting bad behavior.

The Difference between Discipline and Punishment

The strictest definition of discipline is punishment. Punishment has three definitions:

1. suffering, pain, or loss that serves as retribution;
2. a penalty inflicted on an offender through judicial procedure; or
3. severe, rough or disastrous treatment.

Parents should not consider pain, suffering and retribution as an avenue for raising children. As it pertains to children, the definition of discipline parents must use is: Training that corrects, molds or perfects the mental faculties or moral character.

Discipline is synonymous with parenting: The raising of a child by parents. Raising a child means teaching, caring, providing and elevating. Parents must teach the child to survive; care for his mental well-being; provide for his needs and elevate his morals and status in the world.

Keeping all of those tasks in order requires parents to organize their time, knowledge and resources. Discipline is the organizing tool. Many parents profess providing for a child is the easy part of parenting. Merely paying the bills and putting food on the table and clothes in closet is a physical task without many obstacles. Compared to teaching the ways of the world and building moral character in a child, providing for the physical needs is easy.

Developing and implementing an effective discipline strategy is difficult, but not impossible. Every parent has boundaries, a list of things which will not be permitted under any circumstances. Within these boundaries come consequences, what will happen if the child does one of those things. Parents must remember that discipline begins with the list, not the consequences.

So how does discipline become parenting without becoming punishment? Ben Franklin said it first:

"An ounce of prevention is worth a pound of cure."

Franklin knew that making small sacrifices before a crisis arose was always preferable to many reparations afterward. Incremental steps toward building moral character in a child are far easier than correcting misbehavior after it happens. When building a discipline strategy, begin with daily examples of making the right choices.

Teaching a child to share is a simple example of learning complex morality. A child learns to give and take in turn or works in concert by sharing. The majority of societal laws are based on these principles. Sharing demonstrates the concept of ownership, which precludes theft. It illuminates personal space, which precludes violent acts like rape. The seeds of right and wrong are sown early.

Sharing is also a field of choices: what to share, with whom, for how long, under what circumstances. Good decision-making is the most important facet of successful parenting. Beginning with simple choices, like which foods to eat, and graduating to more complex choices, like which courses to take in school, parents mold a child's decision-making to ensure future success.

Allowing a child to make mistakes, bad choices, and letting him suffer the consequences are just as important as any lesson the parent can teach. Pain is the human body's built in receptor to warn of ill action. Instinctively, parents shield their children from pain. It is inconsistent for parents to inflict pain. Here is where the strict definition of discipline is abandoned.

Ridicule, physical punishment and isolation are all painful in their own rights. Children face these consequences every day. Poor choices in apparel garner ridicule from peers. Poor navigation choices on a tricycle produce skinned knees. Poor choices in moral situations beget isolation, either in the form of loss of peers or imprisonment.

Parents need to choose which decisions a child should make to instill awareness of consequences to actions. There is a fine line between what is educational pain and what is abusive pain. Parents need to know the tolerance level of the child and be prepared to intervene before the lesson is spoiled. Remember the lesson of the nesting cups.

When consequences are too harsh, the child's perception changes to that of a victim. They do not perceive their actions as the cause of the consequence; instead feel unjustifiable retribution, which leads to paranoia or fear. Children should not fear consequence, but should learn from it. The reaction must be equal to the action.

Each child is different. Parents begin with what they know: What they will not tolerate. When another personality, the child, is added to the equation, those tolerances change. The original consequences become malleable. One child may respond to being grounded from recreational hobbies for a week, while another may respond equally to being isolated from the telephone for one day.

In toddlers, this equates to a time out or removal of a toy or abandoning an outing. Remember Terry's theory of time (yesterday, today, tomorrow). He cannot recognize *not* going to a social function next Tuesday as a consequence for his misbehavior on Thursday. Consequences must always be within his time frame and applicable to the infraction.

You know your toddler better than anyone else. Use the method best suited for your family. Don't get disheartened if the first time out yields no results. Try a method three times before declaring it a failure. If your little one is particularly stubborn, try five times.

As long as the end result is no further misbehavior, the consequences should not be absolute. Discipline may well have a finite definition. Its practical application cannot.

Beyond Time Out

Dealing with combative toddlers takes psychological mindfulness and prudent cleverness. Ultimately, though, every mother does wear combat boots. Wear them with quiet confidence only when needed. For most instances, you only need to follow your head (helmets optional).

Super Nanny tirelessly puts children into the "Time Out Spot" in a masterful battle of wills. You tried to emulate her all the way down to the poster announcing the toddler jail cell. But what do you do when your toddler insists on drawing hieroglyphics on the prison wall in lipstick?

First and foremost, your child may not understand the correlation between time out and the offense which sets your teeth on edge or scares you into premature baldness.

Second, *Crime and Punishment* was a great book and a decent television program, but was never intended to discipline a toddler. Punishment must fit both the crime and the maturity level of your two-year-old.

Third, time is relative. Terrible Twos are not forever. Learning takes time. Teaching takes the same amount of time, and twice the patience. Forgive your own frustrations by taking enough time to quell them before disciplining your toddler.

Is there life after time out?

Beyond time-out a world of discipline exists to which toddlers can relate. Two-year-olds, and some older children, simply cannot understand the connection between their actions and the time-out chair or naughty spot. So, the question becomes what is an appropriate consequence for toddler misbehavior?

The Cause and Effect Principle

Your toddler has already learned when you flip the switch, the light goes out. This principle can be applied to everything your child does and is commonly referred to as consequences. Showing the connection between the action and reaction teaches your toddler how his behavior affects his surroundings.

You are drawing in coloring books with your child, and he dumps the crayons onto the floor. Sweeping him to the time-out chair with admonishment while you retrieve the crayons does not compute the way you think it might. What your toddler learns is: If I dump the crayons on the floor, I get to see Mom crawl on the carpet like the dog.

Safe to assume, what he learned was not what you were teaching. A better alternative is state your admonishment about the cause and let him feel the effect. "We do not dump crayons out of the box. Help me put them back in the box."

Rather than getting on the floor with him, let him hand you the crayons or simply hold the box for him to replace them. What your toddler learns is: If I dump the crayons on the floor, I have to pick them up.

Unlike distraction techniques, cause and effect should not be sweetened with fun. If the effect is a game, you are reinforcing the bad behavior. He will dump the crayons on the floor to play the pick-up game.

The "If this, then that" Principle

Your toddler has learned if she gets in the bathtub, then she gets wet. This principle applies to situations where your child is directly affected physically by her behavior. It requires specific restraint for parents and is most commonly referred to as learning the hard way.

Parents need to resist the urge to provide a completely consequence-free environment. Do put your great-grandmother's china into the china closet. Do not bubble wrap all of the corners in the house. Occasional trips and falls are the norm in the toddling stage. They teach balance to combat the unpleasant feeling of landing on knees and behinds. Allow your child controlled environments which will not produce great bodily harm, but will exhibit danger.

You are cross-stitching while your child watches television. She is inordinately interested in the contents of the sewing basket. Firmly state: My sewing basket will hurt you. If she persists, show her. Without piercing the skin, show her what the pins in the cushion feel like on her skin. You did not draw blood, but you did teach her some places are prohibited for her own safety. Fortunately, these lessons are learned in one sitting.

Likewise, this principle should be applied to others and objects. Commonly, toddlers will pull the tail or ears of a pet. Explain the yelp to your toddler. "It hurts, just like when you fall down." Use the inverse as well. When he falls, tell him, "This is what the cat feels when you pull her tail."

When a delicate object breaks, let her hold the dustpan as you sweep the pieces. "It is broken, and we have to throw it away." While more difficult to understand than direct consequences, empathy is forming which will guide your toddler to more careful behavior.

The Action vs. Reaction Principle

Your toddler has learned if he has a tantrum, you will not be pleased. His budding emotions are encompassing more complex feelings than the happiness/sadness set of infancy. In his desire to please and thirst for praise, he may miscue on ways to seek your attention.

His developing autonomy introduces feelings of independence and frustration in his failure to accomplish all he attempts. His limited communication skills further frustrate his efforts to educate you on what he is feeling.

When your toddler combines his independence with his curiosity, a bizarre chemical experiment turns into mad science. Unfortunately, it is his science making you mad, figuratively and/or literally. The following example will explain the situation with your prize tulips (Chapter 3).

The Masterpiece

You are washing dishes, and your toddler presents you with a piece of construction paper, covered in three ounces of school glue, half a bottle of glitter and feathers from the duster you inadvertently left in the living room. What he is seeking is adoration and adulation. He has made a masterpiece and graced you with it.

What you are feeling is bordering on rage and causing your eye to twitch. Deep in your heart, the warmth at the present is the emotion which must rule the day to salvage this perfect opportunity for discipline.

In the six nanoseconds after you spied the artwork, you have been through the first two principles and concluded: It will take you thirty minutes to clean the mess, and your back will be sore from getting the glitter off the wood floor.

Smile. "Thank you for making me a picture." Take it away to a safe place. You have rewarded the creativity and giving spirit which are deserved of praise and reinforcement.

Take your toddler to the disaster area. "You made this mess. Help me clean it." Simple, clear, firm statements show your reaction to the mess is not mitigated by your appreciation for his present. These are the beginning steps to "The ends do not justify the means."

Although ends and means is a complex concept, Terry is capable of understanding the feelings are not mixed and do not cancel one another. He is not enough of an effective communicator to understand "but". Be certain you are completely separating the appreciation from the discipline.

Talk to Terry, as you clean the mess, about asking permission or for help and boundaries for items which (in your opinion) need adult supervision. While it does stifle his attempts at surprise, take heart: It stifles his attempts at surprise. On the other hand, it sets the stage for Terry coming to you for your input on situations which arise in the future.

You will revisit the need for this separation of emotions many times during the Terrible Twos and as Terry grows up. Use them all to your advantage. The lessons will vary from simple miscues to complex boundary issues which will affect his interactions with others outside the family unit.

> "An ounce of prevention is worth a pound of cure." Benjamin Franklin.

What Did You Learn?

Parents structure their toddlers' lives as much as possible to reduce the frequency of behaviors requiring discipline. By far, reinforcing positive behavior is preferable to disciplining unacceptable behavior.

Model appropriate behavior for your child. When your boss demands you come to work on a Saturday afternoon, remain calm. To your toddler, this situation is identical to you asking her to eat broccoli before cake.

Breaking bad behavior habits takes far longer than developing good behavior habits. Effectively communicating the correct emotions and consequences are mandatory for success in disciplining a toddler. Despite your best effort, however, you may not be communicating to Terry in language he understands. More specifically, he may understand the language, but read the situation very differently. Take the time to understand what time-out may mean. Consider it from your toddler's point of view:

> When I shared my toys, Dad did the happy dance. He is funny. I want him to do that again. I will share more toys.

> When I drew a picture on the wall, Mom let me play in my room while she washed the wall. Maybe, I should use marker instead of crayon.

Disciplining toddlers must go beyond time-out to be effective over the long term and lead to better decisions. Better decisions mean fewer punishments, which is the ultimate goal of discipline.

Combating bad behavior in toddlers

by Barbara Whitlock

(introduction by Ann Marie)

With all of the independence your little man is strutting, you are bound to encounter some behavior your child must have learned from his other parent. Whether it is a mantra of *no* or the ever-popular *I can't* or even the *piece-de-resistance* tantrum, your toddler will become a terrible alien life form.

The terrible in Terrible Twos is the storied bane of parenthood and the fodder of your parents' dreams while you were a teenager. Have heart. You have not come to the battle unarmed. Your arsenal is growing with tools to revert the alien back into your darling toddler. So, take aim.

Toddler behavior sometimes wears combat boots. But it's best to avoid combat as much as possible. Unfortunately a toddler's emerging assertiveness is met all too often with parents all too eager to assert their authority. Let's outline strategies to avoid such tussles, as well as arm you for necessary battles.

Avoid direct questions which increase chances of a no.

All toddlers resist parents and learn to hurl a "no" your way as often as opportunity allows. Reduce opportunities by not asking direct questions. Honor their sense of emerging autonomy by giving choices: Choices which move the child toward your goals. Examples:

- Would you like to brush your teeth or put on your PJs first while I get your bedtime story surprise ready?
- Do you think it's a day for wearing dresses or pants?
- Let's eat all our food backwards tonight. I usually eat my broccoli first, but tonight I'm eating my chicken first. Which is backwards for you?
- Should we run or skip to the car?
- Shall we sing or hop while we pick up the toys?

The key to avoiding a *no* is to be smart ahead of time. Anticipate the probability of a *no*. Give choices to avert disaster, but choices never work after your toddler is already resisting. If you offer a choice after the "no" you risk exposing your strategy. Beware! Be mindful and proactive.

Know your toddler's temperament.

All toddlers develop a sense of their autonomy from parents. This forms a gradual self-discovery process which continues through adolescence (and sometimes longer for some adults). Yet the way toddlers express this striving sense of autonomy varies depending on temperament. All toddlers are individuals, but for simplicity's sake, let's group them:

Easy toddlers: These toddlers reply well to distraction and love. When they say *no*, they leave a window open. A tickle, a song or an enthusiastic diversion (Want to have a cookie break?) may work. If not, some sympathy can go far. "You're frustrated. Let's try something else for now."

Medium toddlers: These types can blow up or be persuaded either way. Often it depends on other factors. Are they tired? Are they hungry? Tackle those challenges first, rather than the issue they are resisting. See if that helps. Employ strategies for easy or tough toddlers depending on their mood.

Tough toddlers: You know the type - the ones who leave you feeling you can never do anything right. They are hard to win over to your "team". There is a law of physics in this: Tough toddlers seem to inspire parents to respond with toughness. But picture flint on steel: It sparks. Your goal is to melt away the resistance. Bashing in clay or soaking in a bath can do wonders to neutralize a fiery temperament. Also ask yourself: "Does winning this matter for the issue at hand?" Choose your battles.

How to Use Parent Combat Effectively

This chapter encourages parents to avoid combat whenever possible with toddlers. But there are times when you need to take off those soft slippers and lace up your combat boots. If you absolutely must have your child comply, follow these steps:

Prepare yourself mentally: Breathe deeply and soften your brow.

- Don a gentle smile. Subtly flex your muscles.
- Speak calmly, but firmly: "We need to do this now." Don't pause or wait for a reply - move quickly.
- Use your size and strength advantage: Simply scoop up your toddler and take him where you need him to go.
- If it's a matter of staying in bed, keep him there with a firm hold. If it's getting in a car seat, wrestle the buckle in place.

If the issue can't be resolved by mere transport, weigh what must be done. Teeth can be brushed in the morning. Meals can be skipped. Stores can be left behind. Get home and get him in a quiet place like his room. Stand by until he settles, or just out of view if that's what it takes until he is calm.

Nothing more need be said. In fact, using too many words can diminish your authority, because it's easy to raise your tone or have your voice to shake. But firm physical movements speak volumes to a toddler. Plus, they can yell louder and longer than you.

How to Encourage Toddlers to Behave in Public

The comfort and consistency of home life is conducive to good behavior at home. Toddlers know what is expected next. They have tested the boundaries and come to terms with parental limits on subjects like toys, clothes, food and play.

Your two-year-old will try to have cookies for breakfast every day of the week. After sufficient repetition of the parental chorus "No cookies for breakfast", she understands the boundary. She needed to hear the chorus everyday to understand it applied to each day.

When parents remove toddlers to day care, the grocery store or a house of worship, the boundaries are no longer clear to the toddler. By the same thinking that led her to ask on Wednesday for a cookie breakfast which was not allowed on Tuesday, she will test the boundaries anew when outside the confines of home. The elements of place and people change when you leave home. To her, this situation is completely different from home.

Encouraging your toddler to behave in public requires the same discipline which makes her behave at home.

Fall In! ...For Consistency

Are your child's caregivers on the same page? If a child's caregivers are not "on the same page", the road to a happy child will meander through briers and thorns. Consistency is the backbone of a child's safety net and the prerequisite to trust.

Communication is the first hurdle that must be passed in order to ensure that all caregivers are giving consistent care. This is where all grey areas should be delineated, amended and agreed.

Almost anyone can change a diaper or serve an after-school snack, but no one else will provide the exact regimen of discipline and safety requirements (both physical and moral) as a parent...not even the other parent of the same child.

Begin with time structure. This includes schedules for feeding, self-care, hygiene, sleep and play. Estranged parents must agree to a very similar schedule to provide consistency for the child. If the child spends more time in the care of a facility, parents should adopt a similar schedule to the daycare.

If communication is an issue for estranged parents, bear in mind the best interest of the child. The schedule is not about controlling the other parent's life; it is solely about what is healthy for the child. The parent offering the schedule must be willing to bend in some areas, rather than have the accepting parent make all of the sacrifices.

Nannies, relatives and babysitters must understand and adhere to the schedule unfailingly. In the event that they do not, care for the child should be entrusted to someone who will.

Moral structure is more difficult to enforce. Here the parent must choose carefully those who will care for the child. Interview the personnel extensively before placing your child in a facility. Ask questions rather than giving your view to be certain the caregiver is providing his own answers. Legitimate facilities will have no issue with such interviews. Be wary of those that purport no time for this type of interview.

Ask for the television schedule and a list of activities in which your toddler will participate. Voice objections before placing your child in any day care. If you have more than three objections, find another facility.

Structured discipline will be the largest hurdle to overcome. The instructions must be very clear for the caregiver. When the caregiver has doubt, contact with the parent is imperative. When the caregiver substitutes its own judgment for that of the parent: The structure fails.

Be prepared to check your work. Arrive during a caregiver's time, to ensure that events are progressing in order. Pick your child up from daycare two hours early to see if feeding or discipline has occurred appropriately. Come back an hour after your babysitter arrives to see if your child is her focus.

Do your checking soon after a caregiver has taken the assignment. This will ensure that your child is in the safest hands. In the event that they are not, changes must be made before the child bonds emotionally with the caregiver.

Most parents find enough difficulty maintaining consistency within their own households long before they introduce other caregivers into the child's life. Here, failing to plan is planning to fail. Long before you must choose who will care for your child, you must choose how you will care for your child. Your consistency will produce a well-behaved child for whom anyone will wish to care.

The Foundation

Prepare for better behavior away from home. If at all possible, visit the new place she will go before you leave her there the first time. This exposure to the new environment is an awakening for your toddler. She will meet new people, be exposed to new surroundings and develop a comfort level.

If you cannot visit first, prepare her for her new surroundings by talking about it for at least a week. Even though she still has the yesterday, today, tomorrow sense of time, when the big day comes, she will be more prepared.

Fashion a script with small lines and single concepts:

- I am going to take you to daycare on Thursday.
- Daycare has children.
- The children will play with you.
- The teacher's name is Miss Judy.

Each sentence has a word which is in her working vocabulary. She knows what going, children, play and name mean. By knowing the teacher's name before she goes, you are giving her a contact in advance to increase her comfort level.

This comfort level is the foundation for better behavior. Bad behavior is most commonly the result of abrupt change and unfamiliarity or insecurity in a new setting.

Home as a Concept

Home has many meanings. It is a house, a town, a country, a planet. In the world of a toddler, home needs to be a planet.

Sharing is taught at home, but moves to the playground and play group. It should also move to any place you will leave your toddler. Talk about the way you do things at home as the way things are done when you are not at home. "Miss Judy will share her toys with you. Are you going to share your toys with Miss Judy?"

Continue the situational talk about daycare by comparing the things she will do at daycare to the things you do at home. Let her sleep on a nap mat in her room. Sit down with her for snack time. Have a circle time, even if the other members of the circle have faux fur. All of these activities will make daycare an extension of home. She will be less likely to test all of the boundaries again if she knows in advance certain rules will still apply.

The Moment of Truth

When the big day comes, chin up! Be excited! As you get her dressed, tell her about all the fun she will have. When it is time to leave, hug her and wave...then leave. Do not dawdle. If you have a problem with this part, reread "How to Ease Separation Anxiety" (Chapter 4).

The real truth is: Your child will behave for someone else as well as she behaves for you, if not better. Set and keep a disciplined household to keep your toddler from being terrible in public.

Chapter 7

Teaching Responsibility

Responsibility is a tough lesson to teach and to learn. The best way to teach responsibility is through actions. Modeling responsibility to a two-year-old is impossible. A toddler cannot understand the cause and effect of paying a mortgage or the risk/reward of defensive driving.

A toddler can grasp the concept of responsibility for her own actions and rewards for maintaining responsibilities. Remember, she is little. Her responsibility should be as well. Rewards should commensurate with the level of responsibility. Just as different jobs have different wages, responsibilities should be partitioned according to ability and proficiency.

What can a toddler be responsible for doing? A good gauge is to let him try.

Making a PB&J sandwich? Give him a rubber spatula with peanut butter on it, and let him do it. Will he make a mess? Absolutely. Will he eat the sandwich? You better believe it. Are you going to let him prepare all of his meals? Not a chance.

As your toddler begins taking independent steps, foster them. Slowly, begin reinforcing his independence with responsibility. Show your trust in him by giving him tasks he can accomplish. Reward him for completing them satisfactorily. Manage your expectations. How many times did the Wright brothers crash before taking sustained flight at Kitty Hawk? Quality and proficiency come with practice.

Should you assign small chores to toddlers to build self-esteem?

Your independent little one is determined to help you. Many small chores in your everyday life are perfectly manageable for your toddler. Success in any task produces self-esteem by validating capabilities. Think of the pride you felt the first time you successfully got your child to sleep through the night. While this may not have been a small chore, it was a typical responsibility of becoming a parent.

Responsibility must be meted in proportion to your toddler's ability and understanding. Parents have the responsibility of ensuring tasks assigned to toddlers do not overwhelm them. No parent intentionally wants a child to fail. Exercise caution for both physical and emotional safety.

A big part of the argument for and against giving toddlers chores is the size of the job and the quality expected from the effort. Parents' first responsibility is to introduce new tasks with liberal measures of support. Begin by modeling. Enlist the assistance of your toddler. Move to being your toddler's assistant. End with your toddler acting alone.

Each step builds a different element of self-esteem. Modeling builds desire to accomplish and motivates the child to try new things. His best method of discovery has been trying new things himself. Allowing him to help exhibits your trust in his ability. Assisting him when he needs help fosters security. Praise when he accomplishes it on his own finishes the self-esteem cycle by validating his autonomy. Now, he has faith he can accomplish this and other tasks.

Two schools of thought present arguments for assigning chores to toddlers. First, look at the minority, who believe toddlers should not be given chores. Then, read the prevailing arguments for giving toddlers small chores and the reasons these chores build self-esteem. As irony would have it, the arguments are strikingly similar. You have the choice which one is right for you and your toddler.

"No, toddlers should not have chores."

All parents want what is best for their children. The toddler age is filled with growth: emotionally, physically, mentally and spiritually. Living in a loving environment builds the self-esteem during these formative years.

Children learn through play when they are little. Educational programs for toddlers encourage them to explore, sing, discover and play. Through these programs toddlers learn colors and shapes, feelings, and positive self-image is reinforced without placing demands on the children.

Parents have obvious responsibilities, and toddlers love to be near their parents. Toddlers should be allowed to help if they want to help, but parents should not have a specific list of chores a toddler is required to do. During early development, parents should not set up an environment in which toddlers can fail or suffer disappointment.

If toddlers are given a simple chore like pulling up a blanket in the morning when they get out of bed, they will do it in a hurry. Toddlers are constantly on the go and in a hurry. When Mommy disapproves of the job the toddler did, he will be shattered. Or if Mommy gives him the job of folding towels, and she goes back and refolds them after he is finished, he learns his work is not good enough. Toddlers absorb everything from their environments, not just the things parents say.

Leave the toddler years for growing and exploring. Let the older children who already have a positive self-image do the chores. Toddlers have a world filled with "no" just to keep them safe. Accept them for the growing children they are. Parents do not need to put chores on the list to build self-esteem.

"Yes, toddlers should have chores."

Accomplishment

The chores you assign your toddler have less to do with the actual work being accomplished (or if the work gets accomplished) than it has with whether or not your toddler thinks he accomplished something by helping. One parent says:

> Your toddler may love helping you "wash" the car. By this I mean, waving the hose around soaking everyone actually washing the car. As long as your child believes she is helping, praise her for helping. She learns from the chore she's just done something useful.

Terry is perfectly capable of helping Daddy take out the garbage. With Daddy firmly gripping the top of the bag, Terry can single-handedly hold the bulk of the weight in the palm his little hand all the way to the trash can. Chore done, and he helped...like the big boy he is becoming. The celebratory walk back in the house on Daddy's shoulders punctuates the triumph nicely.

It's all about child labor.

Chores can be such an ugly word. Some of the best chores for toddlers are not chores at all. By calling them chores, we set the stage for praising them for how responsible (adult-like) they are acting. At this age, it is the thing they want most to do: gain your praise. One parent says:

> At this age, two-year-olds are eager to please and copy the behavior of those they love. Toddlers think whatever Mommy or Daddy is doing is fun. They want to help.
>
> Parents need to encourage this eagerness. Allow children to help out whenever possible, even if the task is simple. Holding the grocery list during shopping or "delivering" Daddy's newspaper every morning, when praised on completion, give

toddlers a sense of accomplishment and teach the early stages of responsibility.

Now that you are thinking about it, is your toddler doing some chores all on her own? Keep the volunteer spirit alive and take the next step. Ask her if she would like to help next time you catch her watching you do something.

We all live here.

Since toddlers learn a lot by watching you, seeing you tidy up your things in the evening may just tempt her to pick up her toys before bed as well...but don't count on it. Learning to clean up after oneself is a task every person must learn. While some consider this a chore, others consider it personal responsibility. Either way, it is a lesson everyone should learn.

Two is the perfect age to learn this lesson. At two, the lesson can still be taught as a game.

Believe in me.

You already know you cannot fit everything you must do everyday into the time when Terry is asleep. You also know he would rather be doing what you are doing than what you want him to be doing while you do something else. Use this to your advantage.

As you include him in the everyday tasks you do, like household chores, you are teaching him many important principles beyond just cleanliness and teamwork. By allowing him to pitch in, you are showing your faith in his abilities. He needs this affirmation to build self-esteem.

By expecting him to pitch in, you are teaching him responsibility. He grasps the concept he plays a role in the everyday function of the household. He holds status in the home. He recognizes your status as a parent, but now he, too, has a status of his own.

The Reality Check

She is too little to have a chore chart on the wall and an allowance. The phrase *too little*, specifically, means she is too immature. So, when she decides she does not want to help, exercises the authority of her very own *no*, it is perfectly acceptable.

When she wants to help, let her. When she watches, invite her to help. When she settles into the routine, expect her to help. But when she does not want to participate, understand she is playing a game with you and is more than welcome not to play.

Work should not be forced upon any child.

Appropriate chores for a toddler

Who are you? The parent: Not the quality assurance manager. While you will have some measure of quality control with your toddler, you simply do not have the authority to demand perfection. Rather than giving chores which will be reworked by you after the fact, let your toddler have chores she can accomplish with relative success.

The goal is not to employ child labor, but establish self-esteem and teach responsibility and work ethic. Toddler chores are an exercise of "It is the thought that counts." Celebrate the effort. Trying something new is another step toward independence, self-sufficiency and a lifelong commitment to making good decisions.

What are some chores toddlers can accomplish? Helping is first. Being part of a parent's chore is part of getting bigger. Soon, your toddler will be asking to do portions of the job while you watch. Putting clothes into the washer or dryer, sorting silverware into the drawer, carrying items to the car and filling the bottom shelves with groceries are great examples.

I surveyed twenty parents and bring you their suggestions on appropriate chores for toddlers. They fall into three categories: "I want to help," "Help me do it," and "I do it."

The first are where your toddler helps you do your chores, or distract you while you do them. The second is something your toddler does mostly on his own, but still needs an extra hand to accomplish. The third is all his and strictly hands off for you.

"I want to help" Chores

1. After dinner dishes. Let him stand on a stool and splash water or dry plastic dishes and spoons while you do the dishes.
2. Washing clothes. He is the perfect height to place items in the dryer from the washer. You can let him work on his basketball proficiency putting socks in the washer. He will be a big help sorting the dirty clothes.
3. Putting up the groceries. If you are a stickler about your cabinets or you store food where he cannot reach, he can put the canvas bags away as you empty them.
4. Making his bed. You pull up the blankets, and he puts on the pillow and the animals.
5. Dusting. Move the breakables and toss him a cloth. The coffee table is the perfect height for him.
6. Setting the table. Silverware and napkins are a safe bet. You place the dishes and glasses.

"Help me do it" Chores

1. Clean his room. Broken into small pieces, let him do some, and you do some while he is busy with his part.
2. The go bag. He fetches it. You pack it, but he carries it to the car. (Fully explained in Chapter 8.)
3. Snack time. Let him pick it. You open, cut, or prepare it, but let him put it on the plate.
4. Raking the living room. When he has made a tornado of toys on the floor, let him pick up the bulk, but pitch in when he gets sidetracked.
5. Feeding Fluffy or Fido. You measure the food, but let him serve the kibble and the water.
6. Unload the dishwasher. Sorting silverware is great. You put away the knives first.
7. More laundry. Make a game of finding the clean, matching socks.

"I do it" Chores

1. Putting away shoes.
2. Replacing a single toy after play.
3. Putting games back in the box.
4. Dirty clothes in the hamper or laundry basket.

5. Wrappers and papers in the waste basket. Trash he makes should be his responsibility.
6. Wipe the table. All he needs is a wet washcloth.

Whatever the chore, remember to thank your child for all the help. He is learning the value of teamwork. He will begin to recognize when he can help others.

Foster this team spirit in him. He is combining his exploration and his autonomy, while developing responsibility and helpfulness. You are watching his character deepen. The seeds of work ethic are beginning to germinate.

He will volunteer to do more as his confidence grows. Be liberal in your praise for his efforts. The chores will move from the first list to the third list in a flash.

Chapter 8

Coping with New Siblings

It is not easy to lose your status as the star, even if you are a two-year-old. Pregnancy is hard for some adults to understand, much less your terrible two. Think about it from his perspective....

> "Mom's lap is getting smaller. Dad keeps bringing home bags of stuff for the baby...but they aren't for me. Mom sent all my bottles to the babies who did not have any. Why are there new ones now? Dad doesn't think I am really going to wear a dress, does he?"

New furniture is appearing. Some of it may even be in his room. Maybe, he is moving to a new room. Something is afoot, and he knows it. Excitement is palpable. Conversations between adults include words he recognizes: baby, diapers, bottles, crib, little, new.

Then, there is going to be the whole bringing the new baby home day. What's a parent to do?

Developmentally Appropriate Explanations for Pregnancy

Whether you planned it or the pink lines on the pregnancy test were a complete surprise, you are pregnant. Telling your spouse, your friends and even your mother is easy. Try explaining pregnancy and a new baby to a two-year-old. You could lie in bed for hours and not be able to settle on a script for telling Terry he is going to be a big brother.

Don't panic. Parents have been bringing home new babies for eons. Toddlers take to new babies in different ways. Listen to the advice of parents who have ventured into the terrible mine field of announcing a new bundle to a two-year-old who won't share tea with her dolls.

By now, you should be noticing the resonance of similarity between teens and toddlers. Experienced parents know the real differences between them are the cost of their toys and size of their clothes. You may find the best explanation for your toddler is an approach proven to work on a teenager.

Children take adding a new baby to the family in many different ways. Some choose jealousy, some the helper role, still others town crier. Understanding what your child understands about the business of babies is how to determine exactly how to break the news.

Toddlers have a grasp of language, knowledge of the word "baby" and curiosity. Waiting until mom begins to show she is pregnant is usually best, especially since toddlers aren't the most patient creatures. You do not want to be explaining for seven months the baby is not coming home today. Remember, Terry has the "yesterday, today, tomorrow" concept of time.

Engaging toddler in the preparation for baby is essential for smooth transition from being the baby to being the big sister or brother. This is a good habit breaking time as well, since now it is time for baby to have "blanky" or "binky". Letting him place his beloved baby things in the crib is symbolic of not only his growing into big brother but also his first acceptance of the idea of baby.

Elementary school aged children better understand the concept of the baby inside actually being a person. If this child has been the baby for four or more years, take particular care to explain that the new baby will not take her place. Again, allowing this child more responsibility toward care for the infant will reinforce that she is a very valued member of the family.

The ten to twelve year old may be the most difficult to engage in new baby activity. His general tendency to be absorbed by his hobbies and friends will render him almost inconvenienced by mom's pregnancy. If he is not already well-informed, this is the perfect opportunity to discuss from whence babies come and the dangers involved.

With the overall pervasiveness of identity malaise associated with being a tween, he will need a little extra attention, especially just before and after delivery. As you plan your away-from-baby time, make sure to make a date with your tween to go do his favorite activity. This one-on-one time will be essential for maintaining harmony and reinforcing that he is great the way he is.

Teenagers. Let that sink in for a moment. This breed of pseudo-adult will either be thrilled or be totally devastated, likely both on a cyclical basis throughout the pregnancy. Take the happy days as opportunity to shop, decorate or clean. Take the down days to discuss some of the emotional turmoil. You will find it may not have anything to do with new baby at all.

Adult children may be the hardest to tell of an impending sibling. Don't be surprised if the news is met with either sarcasm or humor about the cause of pregnancy or anger coupled with frustration. Tell your adult child as soon as you find out. This is not the time to create trust issues.

Babies are a family event. Share the news. If not thrilled at first, they will love the new baby from the first time they hold it...from toddler to adult children.

Bringing Baby Home

by Barbara Whitlock

(introduction by Ann Marie)

By now, your toddler has a pretty firm grasp on his concept of "There's a baby in Mommy's tummy." Getting ready for baby day is exciting, especially for deliveries by Cesarean section: It is on the calendar, and Terry can mark off the days until the baby's birthday. For the natural delivery moms, baby day is usually a short-notice surprise.

Daddy has been sitting on the couch with your toddler talking about what a big help she is going to be when the baby comes home from the hospital. Her autonomous streak is going to take a huge leap. Easing her into her new role as "big sister" may be as easy as letting her see the baby.

Once in a while, toddlers are not keen on having a new baby once it actually arrives. The preparation for baby day will ease the tension and provide some easy-to-implement solutions to a lukewarm welcome.

The majority of birthing centers offer classes for soon-to-be siblings. These can be a valuable resource for some hands-on input in preparing your toddler for a newborn.

Preparation for Perception

Preparing your two-year-old for a new baby brother or sister requires parent preparation first. And it may require your acting skills as well. A new baby adds much more than plus one to your family life. But your challenge is to pretend like it is simple and easy - no big deal. Why? Your toddler is watching your every move and feels your energy. Here's how to prepare yourself and your two-year old to perceive as minor this major shift in his small universe.

Hide the good news as long as possible.

You've found out you're pregnant again, and you are just bursting to tell everyone. But, don't tell your toddler, and hold everyone to this goal. Why? Nine months is almost half of your toddler's entire life. Waiting that long will be torture; it will feel like an eternity. Fast forward to next week and picture your child asking you seven times every single day until your bring the baby home: "Is the baby coming yet?" You get the picture.

How long should you wait? Ideally, until your child asks, but at least until you start showing. Your child will ask: Why is your tummy so big, mommy? Then, you can tell him about the baby at a stage when he can feel a kick or movement. This grounds an abstract piece of news into something concrete.

Involve big brother/sister in some decisions.

You might say: "This child is two years old -- what can he decide?" Plenty! There are scores of minor decisions to be made: Let him help choose colors for a room, an outfit, bottles, a blanket, etc. His contributions, though minor, invest him in the process of welcoming and preparing for a baby.

Often parents make the mistake of leaving all the baby preparation to talking. A toddler is not a sophisticated communicator, but physical choices he can make and see help him process the upcoming change and feel a part of it. Make it concrete, not just chat.

Do not introduce anxieties not yet named.

Your child will follow your lead. If adding the baby to your family is taken in stride, your toddler most likely will take it in stride. There are exceptions.

Some children, by nature, are anxious. If anxieties arise, never discount them. Always affirm: "Yes, some big brothers and sisters feel like that sometimes. I don't think you'll feel like this after you can kiss and tickle your new baby sister/brother's toes, but if you do you can always tell me about it."

If toddler anxieties persist, make a "then and now" informal book with your child. Have one side of the page be now and what he's feeling in the moment. Then, tell him you will fill in the other side of the pages when the new baby arrives. Most of the time he'll want to put happy pictures on the other side.

Put a lid on relatives and friends who will introduce anxieties for your child, too. Tell them ahead of time how you are approaching this because they need to be focusing equally on Terry's new role. They too will follow your lead. If they will not, end their involvement when Terry is present.

Prepare to integrate the baby into your toddler's schedule.

When you have a second baby, you can't expect to be able to have the leisure time to care for your newborn the same as you did your first child. With no other children you had much more freedom to meet the baby's needs, sleep when the baby slept, etc.

With a second baby you have to work as hard as you can to get the baby to fit in with the toddler's schedule. Yes, it's hard, but be prepared ahead of time.

If you have help scheduled, try to get the helper to help with the newborn more than with the toddler. It will be tempting to do the opposite. But if you prioritize your toddler as much as possible, he will handle the new baby as more of an addition to family life than as a threat to his position.

Save adoring your infant for when your toddler sleeps.

Yes, this is hard, too. All you want to do is gaze in your newborn's eyes, let her body melt into yours, kiss and fondle her. Minimize this focused attention on your newborn while your toddler is watching. Reserve such baby pleasures to your toddler's sleep times.

If your baby and you are locked in a gaze and you see a smile coming, try and connect your toddler to the moment (if he's watching). Say, "I think she's trying to look at you - come closer. Hey, how come she always smiles at you? Being a big brother is pretty special, eh?"

Try to minimize how much you focus exclusively on the baby when your toddler is in striking distance. Instead, deflect those moments away from you toward your toddler. Make him feel in the center of your loving gaze (and the baby's), and not on the outside margins.

Prepare a box of armaments - just in case.

Keep a box of special toys and treats on hand for tricky moments with your toddler. Perhaps, you have to nurse the baby, and your toddler is not too pleased. Introduce the new bath toy, start the bath, and nurse the baby sitting on the toilet if needed, while he splashes. Or set him up at the kitchen sink with the new toy. Water can neutralize anger.

Set up play dough or clay at the table and nurse the baby right there, while he tells you about each thing he is making. Keep your eyes on the toddler as much as possible. Squeezing clay can work out the bad feelings.

Save old watches, a pirate's patch, a bag of plastic cups to build towers and castles. You'll be surprised what can be fun for your child, which costs little or nothing. Add these to the box. Draw out distractions when needed or have your two-year-old close his eyes and pick one.

Food helps too. Before you nurse the baby, ask your toddler if he would like a drink or snack too. Then, he's participating, to some degree, in the nurturing the baby's receiving from you.

Stay calm no matter what.

What's your worst nightmare? Your two-year-old tries to hurt the baby because he's jealous? He screams and develops monstrous behavior because he can't handle the new baby? Just remember: Your child is watching you closely. If you take his reactions in stride, he'll settle more quickly.

Do expect your toddler to regress and want to "play baby" sometimes. If he does, just go with it; don't try and talk him out of it.

- Stick a diaper on him.
- Give him a bottle to drink.
- Burp him.
- Tell him he has to take lots of naps.
- Make him stay in the stroller.
- When he wants a snack, give him a glass of milk only, or baby cereal...fed by you with a baby spoon.

The reality of less freedom and mobility - along with hunger - will persuade him to grow back up, quickly.

Larger-sized families will attest that subsequent children never have a hard time welcoming new babies, because mom having new babies becomes a regular event in their lives. Even though your new baby is the first (or perhaps only) sibling your two-year-old may have to welcome, pretend you're a natural at this.

When in doubt, fake him out.

Acting skills come in very handy: You need to hide the baby's existence as long as possible, pretend like having another baby is "no big deal", and take all of your toddler's behavior in stride.

When he sees how little you are concerned and how much he still gets of your attention, he'll see adding a new baby as simple addition. You can work out all those complex calculations when he's sleeping.

Play along, stick to your script, enlist the acting skills of your spouse and relatives, and orchestrate a score which lulls your two-year-old into thinking having a new baby is barely going to register as a slight change to his regular life.

Building Stronger Bonds between Young Siblings

Young siblings often fall prey to jealousy. For this, the parents are at fault. With even as few as two children, jealousy has no place in your household. Bonding between siblings at a young age is necessary to combat the jealousy.

Step One

First and foremost, parents must realize the new baby is not more important than the older child. Children as close in age nine months can form bonds that lightning cannot break, but only with the help of their parents. The first step is inclusion.

By the time a child can walk, his speech may not be as developed as you would like. It will progress by leaps and bounds by employing the child to help the parent at every stage. When it is time to change the baby, Terry should be fetching the diaper or a box of wipes. This provides vocabulary for him and interaction with baby.

When it is time to go, Terry should be in charge of the "go" bag. "Go" bag should hold only the requisite number of diapers and wipes and one drink and/or snack per child. As baby gets older, your two-year-old will begin to take initiative and fetch the go bag without prompting.

The final stage of this behavior is Terry employing baby (now toddler) in the filling of the go bag.

Step Two

Here is the second phase in the bonding process, which begins once your toddler recognizes the baby is not a replacement model. When Terry can take on the role of example and teacher, he feels as though he is progressing toward the level of parent. Monitor this closely so that Terry does not take the responsibility for discipline.

When baby has playtime, let it be in the room with your two-year-old. This will erase the invisible line between baby and him. Parents will be watching baby play, so incorporating him here is very simple.

If this phase does not naturally begin, you can prompt it by pointing out how Terry's talking and helping is showing the baby how to do things in the same way you showed him. In his mimicry, he will quickly take the responsibility and the chance to be "big".

Step Three

The third phase is amazing and happens without parental intervention. Terry will take on the role of protector of the baby. When baby ventures into a learning experience he has already had, Terry will intervene. He has accepted that this is "his baby" and will not let anything bad happen to her.

Terry will, at this point, begin to recognize baby's needs and alert parents. He will act as interpreter, explaining cries or babbles he thinks you may or may not immediately understand.

You may be surprised what urgency he assigns to baby's cries for food and diapers. He will also be very cognizant of cries of discomfort which you can easily misinterpret. His level of understanding comes from his proximity to the age when he could not speak.

Step Four

The fourth phase is teamwork. Children close in age should act as a unit, much the way that twins do. You will notice that they speak to one another in a language you do not understand. This is perfectly normal and will disappear over time. As Terry takes a larger teaching role, you will find that the younger child will begin to speak and walk earlier than he did.

Time is the crucial factor to this plan. The children must spend time together, both with the parents and, when appropriate, alone. Once parents are sure bullying will not occur, children allowed to play alone together develop games and problem solving skills which just may amaze the onlooker.

Eating together helps form better eating habits and hastens the onset of self-feeding for the baby, who will be mimicking Terry. Do not neglect this quality time spent together. Parents can help themselves by eating with their children to sustain energy.

Where you may want more alone time with your baby, remember that Terry had been the baby first. Close the gap between them rather than widening it. You have the power to build bonds between the siblings which will last a lifetime.

You've brought home a new baby, and your toddler is suddenly talking like one.

You came home from the hospital with the new baby, and your toddler went directly to work fetching needed items and singing to her baby. Slowly, her speech pattern reverts to what it was nearly a year ago. Coos and "dada" return to everyday speech. The little sentences and incessant questions are gone. But, where?

Despite having a rather unnerving effect on parents, this baby talk is merely a return to a familiar time for your toddler. Life as she knew it changed. Just when she thought she had a good handle on how things worked, a new player joined the game. She thought she understood sharing, but she hasn't ever had to share her parents. This is different.

When toddlers are unsure, they revert to the methods they know work. The baby is not talking and still getting everything he needs. As toddler logic would have it, if she talks like the baby, she will get everything, too. This return to baby-speak is a form of tantrum.

While no fault of the parent, it is a matter of perception for the toddler. Parents must change the toddler's perspective with tender care.

Speak to me.

Is everyone who comes to see the baby babbling? Ask them not to do it. Are you doing it? Stop. Do you remember the chapter on "Monkey see-Monkey do"? Set a good example by speaking in the real words you have been teaching your toddler for the last two plus years.

When friends and family come to visit, your toddler can introduce the baby. Teach her to say the baby's name. Let her make some of the milestone announcements.

Especially while you are tending to the baby, talk to your toddler. Talk to her the way you did when you were encouraging her to talk in the very beginning. Narrate what you are doing with the baby and everything else you do.

Don't be afraid to be firm. If she is speaking baby to you, ask her to use her words and talk to you like a big girl. Ask her what the word is.

It's my turn.

Put the baby down, and play only with your toddler. During baby sleep time, take Terry and play something with him which requires lots of talking. Whether it is the naming game (where Terry names everything you can touch) or reading his favorite book and asking him what every single picture is, talk only to him.

This is satisfying two large needs for him. First, you are spending quality time only with him. He has been returned to the number one status he had before the baby arrived. You are melting his insecurity. Insecurity is the reason he returned to the baby-speak.

Second, you are using words with him which you cannot use with the baby. You are making him more special than the baby. Make sure he understands this. He needs to know the baby cries because she is not as big as he is and cannot talk like he can.

Sit down with him and his baby book. Show him he was a baby once, and he got big enough to talk. One day the baby will be big enough to talk and play with him. Talk about all of the games they could play together and the fun they will have. Encourage him to think of things he can do when the baby gets older. Plant the idea he can talk to the baby to help her learn to speak the way he does.

Help me teach.

Your toddler wants to help with everything. Enlist her help in teaching the baby to talk. You know it is far too early to expect your newborn to break into conversation, but your toddler talking to him is not hurting anything. Face it, toddler-speak is a better verbal model than adult-baby-babble no matter how you slice it.

When it is time to feed the baby, why not have your toddler read her favorite book to the baby? Sharing her favorite book is a great way to be a big sister. Playing games, like peek-a-boo or rattling the rattle, with the baby are great ways to encourage your toddler to speak to the baby.

Another easy path back to the words you remember is saying "Good Morning" and "Good Night" to the baby everyday. Even when you know the baby's smile is nothing but gas, make sure you let her know the baby smiled at her.

Chapter 9

Balancing Happy, Healthy & Well-Behaved

What every toddler needs to thrive

All parents want the well-rounded child who is a joy to raise. Although children do not come with manuals, the recipe for a thriving toddler is rather easy to brew.

Everyone knows the basic needs: a crust of bread and glass of water everyday. A stable home and clothing are easy to provide. Formal education is further down the line. Loving parents promote emotional well-being. So, what are the intangibles and the unseen things every toddler needs?

Affection	Hugs and kisses (both plural) every single day and twice as many on Sunday. Say the words: I love you.
Safety	Mobile: Yes. Stable: Not necessarily. Keep him out of danger and poisons safely out of reach.
Approval	Your praise is his currency. It backs up your affection.
Attention	Hours and hours of attention on subjects he thinks are important.
Viability	Just because you do not understand does not mean he is not serious. Take the time to listen to what he has to say.
Mental Stimuli	As the sponge grows, it dries and needs more fluid to absorb. Challenge your toddler by keeping learning activities

and sounds at hand.

Oasis	When Terry rears his head, give him a safe place to cry (or scream) it out. And when it is over, kiss and make up.
Routine	The safety net to know what comes next allows him the freedom to explore.
Socialization	Being with others is how he learns about them, himself and the world. Whether siblings, neighbors, friends or family, expose him to others.
Exercise	To burn off the excess energy he may not have burned growing today.
Naps	The battery is powerful, but needs to be recharged.
Sunshine	Children need the outdoors for many reasons.

This list may look intimidating. In fact, many parts of it are the things you do out of reflex. You are seeing it for the first time as a list.

The first half of the list is the way your personal interaction pays dividends in your relationship. You are helping Terry build character and mature with love and caring. You are giving your toddler what he needs for healthy self-esteem and confidence. These building blocks are the foundation which will support Terry for the rest a lifetime.

The second half of the list is the fruit of your schedule. While it may have a "set it and forget it" feel to it, be certain you are monitoring how well Terry adapts to the schedule. Adjust lengths of activities in both directions, shorter and longer, to ensure both health and happiness.

Small tweaks to it can be the difference between surviving the schedule and thriving under it.

If you find spending time socializing with others is draining the battery to the point a nap will not recharge it, cut out a play date. When lethargy seems to set in and you are certain the battery is not taking a charge properly, try a solar recharge. Sunshine does wonders for both mood and energy.

Play: Why it's so important to a toddler

by Barbara Whitlock

(introduction by Ann Marie)

"Play is the highest expression of human development in childhood, for it alone is the free expression of what is in a child's soul." Fredrick Froebel

You go to classes to learn. Certainly, your toddler is not ready for lectures and a thesis, but he is ready to learn. Mimicry is the greatest tool in his learning arsenal. His fertile imagination makes fun out of the most mundane of tasks. He learns by playing.

Games teach him spatial relationships and the vocabulary to match. He is mastering over and under, in and out. Playing at adult activities teaches him the inner workings of complex problem solving and emotions. Pretending, or make-believe, allows your toddler to express his emotions and how he perceives the world around him. He is learning to mimic others and creating his own expressions.

Parents are a child's first playmates. How do you structure play into your toddler's educational foundation?

Child's Play is Serious Business

"Child's play" suggests something trivial, but children playing is serious business for toddler developmental health. Learn why parents should prioritize play in a toddler's days, and find out the pitfalls if you ignore this priority.

How Toddlers Spend Their Days

United States Census statistics affirm over 65% of toddlers in the US spends six to eight hours per day in daycare or preschool environments. Add in the shocking statistics about average daily television watching: Children watch an average of four hours of TV per day.

Let's do the math:

$$8 + 4 = 12$$

Twelve hours of organized school time plus deadening TV time. When do they play?

The consequences of such TV-viewing patterns are well documented: Alarming rates of childhood obesity, violence, anxiety, ADD, ADHD and autism-spectrum behaviors all point to the same television demon.

Let's take a look at the other six to eight hours a day for the 65% plus toddlers in daycare: They wake early, get ready for school, eat a quick breakfast and get dropped off a daycare or preschool. Time there is highly structured. Play time may be sandwiched between learning, napping, snacking and transitioning between activities. Next, it is home for dinner to bedtime. Squeeze in four hours of TV, and there's nothing left.

Why play is important

Play is vital to a child's intellectual, social and psychological development. Play is a way of structuring, ordering, sorting, imagining and exploring. Using stacking toys gives a child a sense of proportion. Building things out of blocks teaches balance, coordination and stimulates spatial understanding. Imaginative play builds social and language skills, stretches the imagination and expands intelligence.

Through play children explore, talk and connect -- both with others and with themselves. With others they learn how to plan, coordinate, be flexible, think quickly, pretend, act and envision. "I'll be the bad guy - you be the good guy. I'm going to chase you now..." "Let's be spies in the jungle. Tigers try to catch us, and we get bitten by a bad snake." "I'm a princess, and you need my magical powers to be brave and fight the dragon."....the list goes on, the scenarios endless.

Children also need play to sort through their experiences, express their fears and upsets and explore their psychological insides. After parents squabble, you may see your toddler yell at his bear and put him in time out. He may play act hitting and getting in trouble. Of course, he plays the grown-up role in that scenario: He determines the punishment to mete out to the offender, providing a perfect mirror to view your own discipline successes and failures. Grandparent dies, and his animals all line up for a funeral, to bury the toy monkey. Play is a means of expressing sadness, frustration and fear. It restores inner harmony and improves psychological wholeness.

Through play children develop intellectual skills, socialize and grow in emotional intelligence. Without it they will not be as smart, well-socialized or emotionally integrated.

How to Ensure Your Toddler Gets Enough Play

You have the ability to ensure Terry's schedule has enough play time. Take it step by step to offer enough opportunities to play to balance out the structured times in your two-year-old's schedule.

Un-Schedule

Open up the schedule to allow for more free play. Prioritize play in their days. If they are at home let the morning be open to play. Don't schedule classes, doctor appointments, etc. Wake up earlier for play before daycare.

Entertainment

Turn off the television -- or, better yet, throw it out! No toddler needs to watch television. Don't let him use the computer either. No toddler needs to learn to play computer games. Keep plug-in devices off his radar. If you do choose TV, limit to one 30-minute toddler video a day. Don't use regular broadcast television because the shows never stop, and enticements keep them wanting more.

Toys

Buy open-ended toys: dolls, blocks, stuffed animals, dress-up clothes. Avoid an overabundance of toys which do only one thing (convergent toys), that limit the imagination.

Limit the number of toys in your house: Let there be open spaces for play, uncluttered by too many toys. A few stuffed animals, blocks, balls and dress-up clothes are sufficient.

Exercise

Spend a lot of time outdoors. Be outdoors with your children as much as they need. Fence in an area of the yard where toddlers can play safely, and you can watch from the window, too. Make sure they spend several hours outside every day, preferably two or three times each day.

Even in bad weather, use raincoats, boots and rain pants to make rainy days accessible. Get them all they need to go out in cold weather, too.

Daycare

If you must put them in daycare, choose one that allows for plenty of free play time. Over-structuring a toddler's day is detrimental to his health.

Socialization

If you can be at home with your child, take advantage by limiting his transitions and structured time, so he has loads of playtime. If you don't have other children for him to play with, cultivate a friend or two. He only needs to learn how to socialize with other children in small bits, not large chunks.

Don't overdo play with other children. Children don't need much socialization with other children until age three, and then only on limited bases. Once per week or every other week is sufficient.

The Bottom Line

Play is the air children need to breathe to grow, evolve, mature and make sense of the world around them as well as their evolving inner world. To deny sufficient playtime is to risk inadequate intellectual, social and psychological development for children. For toddler's sake, let 'em play!

Nutrition

Toddlers are energy balls buzzing around the house. Some are hugely picky eaters. Others will eat anything that doesn't bite back, and some things that do. Unraveling the mystery of what toddlers need to eat is not difficult. Getting those foods in them just might be.

Nutritional Intake

Every little stomach is different, but the following guidelines are what the National Institutes of Health recommend toddlers eat each day to stay healthy. Mix and match ingredients to ensure the proper total amounts per day.

Grains

Three ounces: At least one half of the grains should come from whole grain sources. Some examples of whole grains for your toddler are whole wheat crackers, whole wheat bread, whole-grain cereal (oatmeal or shredded wheat) or brown rice.

Vegetables

One cup: Vegetables can be raw or cooked. At this age, your child may take three or more attempts before he is willing to eat a new food. Don't give up because vegetables are great sources of vitamins and minerals he needs. If you cannot manage to get him to eat vegetables properly, keep reading.

Fruits

One cup: Snacks and meals can be made more colorful with vitamin filled fruits. Fruits will also fill the natural sweet tooth your child sprouted while you weren't watching. While juice is an option for fruit, it lacks the fiber and much of the vitamins whole fruits possess. Choose fresh, frozen or dried fruits with no added sugar. When choosing juice, always choose 100% juice over juice cocktail.

Dairy

Two cups: Milk and dairy products, like yogurt and cheese, are important for your toddler's bone health. Milk supplies potassium, calcium, vitamin D and protein. You should be giving your toddler low fat or no-fat (skim) milk. Lowering the fat intake is important for heart health and maintaining healthy cholesterol levels, which are more of a concern in children than ever before.

Do not let your toddler drink more than a quart of milk per day. Excessive amounts of milk will inhibit the absorption of iron, which your child needs for energy and to combat anemia.

Proteins

Two ounces: Lean meat, poultry, fish, eggs, nuts and dried beans are sources of protein needed for your toddler's growth and development. Stay away from meat high in fat and cholesterol for heart health. Remember, prepared lunch meats are often high in sodium and fat. Avoid them whenever possible.

Oils

Three tablespoons: Polyunsaturated or monounsaturated fats (good fats) are part of a healthy diet and are a good source of vitamin E. Since they are very calorie-laden, your toddler does not need much. These fats come from nuts, fish (salmon or trout), seeds and oils made from nuts or seeds like peanut, olive, canola or soybean oil.

Supplements

Toddlers eating a variety of foods, fruits and vegetables are not likely to need a supplement. If your child refuses to eat one or more food group, consult your pediatrician before putting your toddler on a vitamin supplement.

Allergies

If your family has a history of food allergies or asthma, most physicians recommend waiting until age three before introducing peanuts, fish and tree nuts. Most food allergies are traced back to five main groups of foods: eggs, milk, wheat, soy and peanuts. Strawberries, citrus fruits and shellfish are other foods known to give allergy symptoms.

Food allergies manifest symptoms ranging from mild to life threatening, including:

- Rash, eczema and/or hives
- Respiratory distress such as sneezing, wheezing, coughing and nasal congestion
- Digestive distress such as vomiting, diarrhea, constipation and abdominal pain

Since these symptoms are indicative of many other ailments, they should be discussed immediately with your toddler's pediatrician. Seek immediate emergency medical attention if your toddler has trouble breathing.

Doctors will test to pinpoint the food allergy. While a peanut allergy is most easily solved by avoiding peanut products, milk or wheat allergies require the help of a dietitian to plan a diet to meet the nutritional needs of your toddler.

Tricky Ways to Add Nutrition to Food

"If you knew what was in it you would not put it in your mouth."

The fact of the matter is: We do know what is in it, and we eat it anyway! So why not make that a healthy choice rather than a cholesterol- and calorie-laden one?

Research is showing high cholesterol is appearing in more children at younger ages. Take the time to cut as much cholesterol out of their diets as possible. Replace it with healthy vegetables.

Is that easier said than done? Here are some top notch ways of introducing vegetables into everyday foods for children (and even teens and adults), who would starve before succumbing to a floret of broccoli.

Spaghetti & Pasta

My husband likened eating whole wheat pasta to chewing ground glass. Ironically, spinach and carrot pasta (usually rotini) meets with approval. The triglycerides of Durham pasta are the #2 culprit for high cholesterol.

If you cannot go to whole wheat, at least you can change from Durham to veggie. Children find the colors and shape of the veggie pasta interesting and fun. Forget the sauce and the spoon. This can be a finger food with a light dusting of grated Parmesan and/or a drizzle of extra virgin olive oil.

Sauce

Ah, the hider of many vegetables! I must confess: I got caught. I was avidly chopping carrots into oblivion when my husband found the kitchen for a drink. After three years of never having a clue, he discovered what I had been doing.

Everyone can use more beta-carotene. Add tiny pieces of carrot (Beet is better.) to the sauce at the beginning. They will dissolve. You are wiser, and they see better.

Don't stop there. Mangle a mushroom. Iron does a body good. Cut one or six into matchstick pieces. The mushrooms which do not completely dissolve will resemble (and taste) like meat in the sauce. Toadstool shaped pieces are picked out, but tiny pieces are devoured. Use Portobello when you can find fresh ones, buttons when you can't and shiitake every time.

Have you noticed that pizza has sauce on it? Veggie pizza gets all thumbs down, doesn't it? Make your sauce pack more punch.

Meatballs

Hide the spinach! Fresh chopped spinach looks like parsley when added to meatballs. Don't tell, and they will never know the difference. Throw in some crushed carrot or use two ounces of pure carrot juice in place of some of the tomato sauce.

Pass the peppers, too. Bell and banana peppers don't add heat, but add vital nutrients, like vitamin C, to every dish. Toss in some olive bits (black and green)...very good for you.

Chili

You have the carrot theme by now. Toss in some oddly shaped pumpkin pieces or stir in a cup of packaged (not spiced) pumpkin. It will add depth to the sauce without sweetening. Use fresh onion, rendered before you add it. Better flavor is a bonus when you consider the added iron. More toadstools are disguised in this dish for a power boost of iron.

Chicken Casserole

If they will pick out a piece of veggie, make it invisible. Prepare cauliflower before you start. Crush it into a paste with chicken broth to add to the canned cream soup. My children will swear that they never eat cauliflower. The joke is on them!

Pesto

Green is usually more difficult to hide. Try squeezing some peas into your pesto when you slip in the fresh spinach. Although the peas will sweeten the pesto slightly, the spinach will not. Arugula will take away the sweet, if you find some at the market. Better still are beet greens. They have a peppery taste with a hint of sweetness that hides well in pesto.

Salad

If they eat salad, you have won the first battle. Win the coup. Scrape the flowers off the broccoli florets with a spoon. They are too small to pick out of the salad dressing. Add different greens: spinach, kale, beet greens, arugula, Romaine hearts, mustard greens, and red cabbage. Stop buying iceberg lettuce altogether. Smaller pieces mean more eaten with less ability to remove the goodness. Use the tips outlined above to beef up the salad.

Don't be shy. Feel free to drop a piece of fruit, or seven, in the salad as well. Skin a few orange segments, dice a Granny Smith apple or toss in some mango cubes. Fruit does a body good. Add some natural crunch with a handful of nuts (walnuts or cashews) or seeds (sunflower or sesame). Skip the croutons in favor of natural crunch.

Guacamole

Holy moly, what you can hide in guacamole! Don't try hiding leafy veggies here, but crush some lima beans. I am not crazy: This works. They have the same texture beneath the skin as an avocado and are equally receptive to the spices you add. Did I mention that they are exactly the same color?

Juice

Adding juice to any dish (in the place of water) will add vitamins. Adding juice to juice makes just as much sense. My house thinks I like carrot juice: Silly rabbits! Carrot juice is for kids! Half a cup added to pitchers of powdered drinks (Kool-Aid or Gatorade) is never detected by the troops.

Find the nectars, which come in aluminum cans, in your juice aisle. Add these whole fruits in places you would sugar a dish to add healthy calories instead of empty ones.

Yogurt

Now, you already know yogurt is good for you to start. Let's add some punch to it. Add fresh fruit to it. Instead of the fruits your child already eats (apples and bananas), add the ones with different vitamins he may not eat: peaches, mangoes, pears (in small doses), passion fruit or pineapple. Introducing tropical fruits through yogurt and juices is a great way of widening his palate while you infuse vitamins.

Pear has a natural laxative effect. Offer pear in only quarter-cup servings and then only every other day. If your toddler is constipated, pear nectar or a half cup serving of pear pieces will naturally ease the problem without harsh chemicals.

Smoothie

Blend up a banana, an organic yogurt, some frozen berries, a tablespoon of wheat germ and a healthy spoonful of flax seed oil. The wheat germ is a healthy way to add interesting texture. Mix and match ingredients you know your toddler likes with ones he may blatantly turn down when offered solo. This is another great place to use nectar to add sweetness or a different or out-of-season fruit flavor.

Cake

Yes, nutritious cake. A spice cake is the perfect place to hide carrot or zucchini shreds, if you want to stick to the tried and true. With a cream cheese icing, veggie cake is a dessert you can offer for breakfast.

If you like adventure, try some inventive cakes. Instead of adding pudding mix for added richness, try blended fruit (skin included) or berry sauce. Substitute mango nectar or pureed banana for oil. Crush nuts and blend them in cream cheese frosting for a double boost of dairy and protein. Children never look for nutrition in dessert. Oh, let's be honest...No one looks for nutrition in dessert.

Formula

If your toddler is just outright picky and none of the rest of these ideas (besides adding juice) is working to get him back on the path of healthy eating, go back to the baby section and buy a can of powdered formula.

This is a complete source of balanced nutrition. It has an advantage over those pre-made nutrition drinks in the pharmacy section, too. It does not contain any added sugar or unnecessary salt.

While you may not think toddlers need to be watching salt intake, they do. Salt toughens the gums, which makes breaking in their new choppers tougher on them, and consequently you.

By adding a scoop (two ounce equivalent) of formula powder to every cup of milk, ice cream, smoothie and yogurt, you will see your toddler head back in the direction of better growth and health.

I know it is sneaky, but I got these ideas when I had the eyes installed in the back of my head. *I have ways of making you eat your vegetables!*

Weight concerns

by John McDevitt

(introduction by Ann Marie)

Each play group has the one toddler who has not outgrown his baby fat. Pediatricians can give you charts and graphs and pamphlets on what children should weigh and when. Despite the mountains of information, parental instinct cannot be discounted.

Many factors will affect the weight of your toddler: Calorie quality and intake amount, activity level, genetic structure and family history. The time has come to lay groundwork for a lifetime of healthy eating habits and nurture a love of exercise. Making it fun is a great method of expanding a toddler's dietary choices without tipping your hand that these new foods are good for her.

Good nutrition takes sacrifice, especially for parents who do not have good eating habits themselves. Parents must be particularly careful not to inadvertently "pass down" dislikes for vegetables and other nutritious foods. Allowing a toddler to discover likes and dislikes is as simple as putting only good food on the plate in the correct quantity and letting her see the whole family enjoying it.

Food is no substitute for a big hug.

Fast-forward fifteen years to the image of a confused, obese teenager, sitting alone hugging a huge bag of chips for comfort and company. It can happen when parents substitute food for love.

Strong emotions and food don't mix. Fighting and forcing your toddler to eat new, unfamiliar food is the flip side of using food as reward and comfort. Neither one works, and both develop unhealthy attitudes which can warp a child's eating habits for life.

Toddlers are learning machines. Everything they see, hear, feel, touch and taste plunges them into a new adventure.

Eating is no exception. They'll carry the eating habits and food attitudes they learn as toddlers throughout their lives.

Food should be used to ease hunger and nourish the body, not the emotions. Give an upset toddler a treat to calm them or rail at them because they refuse food they should eat, and they're likely to develop an unhealthy emotional association with those foods. Food should be a pleasure for toddlers, not an emotional battleground that will haunt them all their lives.

Make eating and mealtime a normal, everyday experience for your toddler. It's the best way to teach them good eating habits. Toddlers are unsteady on their feet. Like walking, eating is a new experience for them. Be easy. Don't expect your toddler to become an instant good eater. Toddlers can be the most stubborn creatures on earth. Arm wrestling them into submission won't work. Show them instead.

Tell a toddler that they should eat something because it's good for them, and you're likely to get a blank stare. A person (Toddlers are people, too.) will only eat food they enjoy. Be honest. Would you eat something because someone told you it was good for you? Toddlers won't either.

Toddlers mimic what they see. When they see the family enjoying a healthy balanced meal, they'll begin to eat what you eat. Never force a new food on them. Give them time. They probably won't like the first taste, but when they watch you and the rest of the family enjoying their food, your toddler might try it again next time.

Hint: Take a good look in the mirror. If they see you eating junk, then junk must be good, and they'll want the same junk. While you're looking in the mirror, examine your own eating habits and attitudes about food.

Step back and look carefully. Are mealtimes a pleasant family experience or contentious and unappetizing? Do you serve healthy food or feel good comfort food? Do you use sweets as rewards? Do you snack in front of the television?

Early feelings and attitudes about food will follow your toddler for life. Turning to food for comfort or reward can easily lead to childhood obesity and become a lifelong weight problem for your child. Emotional aversions to certain foods born of fear and strife are just as unhealthy. It doesn't need to be that way. Your good example and patient understanding are the best teachers.

Chapter 10

Parents' Successful Survival

Parents reflect on The Terrible Twos

Do you remember this book assuring you that the Terrible Twos are not forever? Now, the truth is bared by parents who have survived the Terrible Twos. Some have come to this place for the first time. Others have been there more times than they care to admit. Some have been through it with more than one generation.

You will discover the fun two-year-olds deliver at regular intervals. Share the laughter with other parents who see the divine humor in toddlers. Find out toddlers can be smart enough to scare you at times.

Most of all, know you, too, will survive the Terrible Twos.

by John McDevitt

I danced at their weddings and held their newborn babies. I watch their daughters (our granddaughters) grow into young ladies. Time rushes in reverse as I view the so called terrible twos through the eyes of a sibling, a proud parent and a grandparent.

My sister Mary took over the decorating not half an hour after the wallpaper guys finished and left. Mary only wanted to help. She took her crayon and made her creative contribution on every wall in the house until my heartbroken mother caught her in the act. "What did I do wrong? I was only helping." Mary became the terrible two poster child after that one.

It's my way or the highway. My oldest discovered it was the highway for her. Imagine a shopping cart filled with groceries with a kicking, screaming two year old in that cart. "I want that!" Nope. Picture a shopping cart filled with groceries sitting abandoned in the middle of the aisle and a shocked two year old plopped into her stroller on the way home empty handed.

I can't remember why I left the bathroom door open that day. I think I was afraid to leave her (my oldest again) alone but I had to pee so bad and needed to hear what was going on. "NO, don't stick your hand in there! Stop you'll get all wet!" Yeah, she stuck her hand in the stream and... I can't remember the rest but it was a mess. Hey, she was exploring her world.

It's been a long time now, but I'll never forget the screams for help coming from upstairs. I raced up the steps and found my youngest (We have two daughters.) holding back the dresser that threatened to come crashing down on top of her. Don't ask how that happened. We couldn't figure it out either.

One day my oldest daughter broke the slats while jumping on her sister's bed. She fixed it so it looked normal and when Sue got on her bed later and it collapsed, she was hysterical because she thought she did it.

Terrible twos or a chick cracking the egg in the struggle to emerge as a person? *I am me. See me, watch me, love me, protect me but let me be me -- please?* They flex their newfound toddler muscles, exploring, learning, testing you and your patience. We're guardians and protectors, not owners or prison wardens. We try to strike a balance (and not the kids) between overindulgent and tyrant wondering if the terrible twos will ever pass. They don't.

The terrible twos give way to the thrilling threes and the ferocious fours all too quickly. Doors kicked in because they wouldn't open, tantrums because they didn't get the Christmas gift they wanted, hard objects hurled at a teenage sibling, door closed in the nick of time so the bedroom door had the hole in it instead of a head.

Then one day she and I, that terrible two, walk down the aisle together, she holding on for dear life, wedding veil trailing behind, me holding her up. Then later, dancing and celebrating. The wheel turns again as our daughters give birth and become protectors, safeguarding the future -- all too soon dancing at their daughter's wedding.

by Tina Hartley

Habitually, I glanced at the clock as I headed towards the ringing phone. It was five minutes after nine. "Hello, Harvard Lodge," I said. "This is Tina, how may I help you?"

Susie's voice shrilled with panic on the other end, "Tina, I can't find David!"

Being naturally cool-headed under stress, and knowing my darling 20 month old child, I said "Calm down, Sue! Are the doors all closed?"

"Yes, yes! I looked everywhere. I don't know what to do! Oh my God, Tina, I'm so sorry! He's gone! He's just gone!" she nearly screamed into the phone.

Thank goodness there were no customers to deal with at the moment. "C'mon, Sue," I said as gently as I could, "You know how Davey is. Let's take this one step at a time. Is the toy box open or closed?" I knew one of my son's favorite places was inside the toy box with the lid closed.

"It's open, Tina. I checked there already" she said, sounding slightly less hysterical. Susie had been my babysitter for nearly six months. She was great with David. She was great with all three kids. She had never been daunted by my little handful, unlike her two predecessors. I just had to help her get calmed down. I mentally went through my home thinking about where David's favorite places were.

"Is Jamie sleeping?" I asked. The oldest of my three children, he had school in the morning. He should be snug in his bed by now. "Yes, he's sound asleep," Sue said. I had been hoping for a negative answer.

Jamie knew his little brother so well, he could have been a big help. "Is Ray there?" I asked. Sue's boyfriend, Ray sometimes helped her at night. He was good with the kids, too. Ray always said "Dave's not just a job, he's an adventure!"

When Sue indicated Ray was there I asked her to send him on a perimeter check. I knew Davey wasn't afraid of the dark but I really didn't think he would wander far at night with everyone else in the house. "Tell Ray to make sure to check the garage," I said. I sent Sue to check in the hall closet. He wasn't there. "Look behind the washer," I said. Davey had recently discovered he could fit behind there. I suggested she check in the dryer. Sue said she had checked there already.

I was really stretching now. It seemed most of David's most infamous spots had been checked already. I asked if she had checked under all the beds. She said she had. "Start opening each bottom kitchen cabinet one by one," I instructed her.

About two minutes passed before I heard a scream of delight from Sue. "I found him! I found him!" she squealed. When she picked the phone back up, she said "He was in the cabinet by the refrigerator, sound asleep!"

I smiled and said, "Put him in his bed, Sue. I really need to get back to work." Sue started to apologize for bothering me at work, but I cut her off. "It's okay. You're the greatest, Sue. I see you when I get home."

Davey was indeed an adventure! As I finished my work over the next two hours, I thought a lot about Davey. He was such a happy child, so full of energy. As he neared his second birthday, it was necessary for me to re-think everything I thought I knew about toddlers.

Driving home from work that night I resolved to get cabinet locks. I hadn't kept anything toxic in lower cabinets for years, since Jamie had started crawling, but there were still things that Davey could get hurt on. I didn't care to imagine the damage a falling cast iron skillet could do to a tiny foot. I had never needed locks for Jamie. A firm "no" had steered him away.

Jamie had been a rather quiet child. When he was a toddler, he had shown some minimal defiance and few temper tantrums. Davey was showing signs of making up for the ease of parenting Jamie through the terrible twos. Two weeks earlier, I had sheepishly purchased a child harness. I was horrified when I saw my first child harness. I thought of it as putting a leash on a child as treating him like a pet.

With David, it was a matter of safety, period. He was so quick! If I turned my head for 60 seconds, he could be anywhere by the time I turned my head back. I was afraid to not have him tied to me in public. I worried about him darting into traffic, or even being grabbed by a stranger. He simply had no fear of anyone or anything.

It was obvious I was going to need to try entirely different tactics with David if he and I were going to survive the next year, or two. Through a lot of trial and error I found distraction to be what worked the best. It seemed the word "no" meant "go" to Davey. Where my voice or just a look had been enough to re-direct Jamie, I seemed to be invisible to my younger son when he was intent on something.

I still gave a firm "no" when my son was trying to scale a bookcase, or pull the dog's tail, but a redirect was always needed with it. I steered him towards something fun and safe at the same time. He wasn't really defiant so much as he had a one track mind. Thankfully, his temper tantrums were few and far between. He didn't get frustrated very often. He just kept going like the Energizer bunny.

When he did throw a tantrum, it was a sight to behold. He would kick and scream and throw things. There were times when I had to physically wrap him up in my arms to keep him from hurting himself, or someone else. I separated him from whatever was upsetting him, and once he was calm again, we went together to face his nemesis. Often it was a broken toy that wouldn't do what he wanted it to.

My presence seemed to help keep him calm. I kept a running commentary as we worked together on the broken toy. I explained what I was doing and had him hand me tools as I worked. I know he didn't understand everything I was saying, but making him a part of what I was doing seemed to help him understand enough. The one thing I learned early from him; if I lost my patience, he did too. Staying calm and softly talking to him helped him and me through it.

The outdoors and fresh air seemed to be the best medicine for my little bundle of pent up energy. I took him outside to play for several hours a day, weather permitting. When I couldn't be with him, I instructed my sitter to do the same. It seemed playing outdoors helped him to burn off some of his incredible energy. Fortunately, we had a large yard with plenty of child safe places to explore. On the days when the weather kept us inside, the hobby horse was his favorite place. He could "ride" some of his energy away.

David had taught me as many things as I had taught him. My two sons couldn't have been any further apart in personality. Before David, I had thought once you raised one child through the toddler years you were ready for the next one. David quickly and decisively corrected that complacency! He forced me to think outside the box and be creative. Most of all he made me realize just how much my emotional state affected his. I couldn't demand his cooperation. The best I could do was to use my calmness to help him find his own.

I reflected on the "terrible two" days as my son and I waited for the school bus. I wondered if he would balk at getting on the bus without me on his first day of school. As the bus pulled up at the bottom of our driveway and the driver opened the doors, he cheerfully climbed on without a look back. My fearless son had no qualms about heading off for new adventures. I was the one who was having separation anxiety. A tear slid down my cheek as I waved good-bye. The house would be so quiet without him.

by Barbara Whitlock

I'm a teacher at heart, whether caring for my brood of five girls, teaching in prep schools, serving up my unique writing curriculum, homeschooling my own or others', or adding to Helium.com's writing community. Teaching is not a top-down phenomenon to me, but a dynamic process where teacher and learner fuel a learning dynamism that buzzes with electricity and hums with expectant energy at unpredictable intervals. The world is such a curious place, and people present even more complexities -- our children most of all. Puzzling it all out makes for a rich life, marked by continuous (and humbling) growth, as well as evolving enlightenment.

I knew myself as a writer first at age ten, when my sixth grade teacher, Mrs. Johnson, signed my autograph book and wrote: "To a girl who has a flair for writing." I soared when I read that; and the clarity of my memory -- almost four decades later -- provides further testimony. So often we became aware of a drive within us, but it takes someone else naming it to reach conviction. I've never stopped writing since that point. And no matter what I've been "doing" in life, my writer awareness watches, primed. It also seems word-craft has always worked its way into my various jobs. I'm currently birthing a book: *The Homeschool Refuel Book: Strengthening Parents for the Longer Journey.*

For the past 15 years, my primary focus has been my children, who now range from very young adult, teens to pre-teens, and one sort-of child, who aspires to catch up quickly with her older sisters. I was raised with mostly girls (four sisters plus one lone brother), and I've birthed five girls of my own. We've now transferred diaper purchases for menstrual pads; but no matter heights or curves, they remain big babies underneath it all. And they still need their mama, in one form or another.

I'm convinced that if parents can gain true enlightenment dealing with toddlers they can handle any teenager on the face of the earth, and they set the stage for healthy relationships with their adult children.

Toddlers strain for self-identity, a sovereignty of self that lies a toddler-stride away from parents' side. Teens, especially those who drive and go off to college, go further, but the pulls remain the same. Parents are attached -- and usually mamas most centrally -- with an expanse of elastic between their hearts (and bodies) and their children's. The invisible elastic merely replaces the former umbilical cord. And the connection is just as real, even when a toddler or teen screams "no!"

If parents shepherding toddlers "get it" about that natural drive to explore a more expansive world, and recognize the unique sovereignty in each of their kids, then they pave the way for a perfect balance between healthy attachment and secure independence in their children. All too often parents feel they need to assert their "authority" and "control" the situation so kids know "who is boss".

In fact, the only real boss is God: The rest of us are here on Earth trying to get it right. We get it right best when we respect each other's being with great humility, and we guide with gentleness, reserving our authority for the respect earned through service and wisdom. That doesn't mean we don't have to get down and dirty with our kids and hold to the firm boundaries that clarify order and assure harmony. But we can hold the line without losing our hold on the sacredness and individuality of our children (and without losing our cookies).

God blessed me with the most cantankerous first born anyone could meet. He prepared me for this the very first moment she emerged into the light. Previously, I'd been to parenting classes where the instructor told me "you'll need time to get your know your baby." I thought "balderdash, she's a part of me -- I already know her."

And then she was birthed, and the nurse held her up for me to see. Her dark eyes were wide open. She didn't cry at all. She just stared right at me, a stare that seared like an electric shock through my entire central nervous system. I spontaneously exclaimed: "Who are you?!" It was at that moment that I touched the root humility that her every year has reminded me: She is a being totally distinct from me, though inextricably connected. My other four girls have given me ongoing lessons to reaffirm this primal lesson.

Over the years I've realized that parenting is about humble service to the uniquely created creatures that show up at our breasts and remain forever in our hearts. Yeah, we have to say "no"; we yell on occasion; wring our hands and cry up to the heavens about them. But, if we get it right, we fall down on our knees, see them straight in the eye, and we grow tall in wisdom right along with them -- and, if we're lucky, one step ahead.

by Melanie Denyer

At times, as I've thought about what I would write, I've felt a complete fraud discussing the so-called terrible twos. Yes, I have a little boy who has just turned three, and I'm certainly qualified to speak about that period of his life but, in all honesty, it really wasn't that terrible.

Not that I am making my son out as some paragon of all youthful virtue, either. Tantrums? Check. Stubborn? Check. Mischievous? Check. Downright naughty on occasion? You bet. But I have not spent the last year praying for his third birthday the way I thought I would when he threw his first tantrum in the middle of a supermarket. Far from it.

I entered motherhood on a tide of hormones, confident that it would all come naturally, like the desire to have kids in the first place. The first few months were fantastic, barring a milk supply problem that we eventually solved by switching him to formula. But taking care of my newborn really was second nature, and I could tell from the first cry what was wrong on a given occasion. I was totally besotted with my little boy and grateful beyond belief that he was so easy-going.

Of course, kids do get older, and Harvey was no exception. He was still happy and outgoing and co-operative right up until his first tantrum, but the older he got, the more difficult it became for me to care for him. That instant understanding of his every need was gone, and his little will was gearing up to assert itself more readily.

It was at this point that I realized all hope of being a natural mother was gone. I had to face it. There are women who seem born to raise children and throw themselves fully into that role, who find it the most fulfilling thing they could ever do. I'm not one of them. Worse, suffering from chronic depression and perhaps over-conscious of the effect that might have on my son, I was afraid of engaging too closely. It wasn't that I didn't love him, just that I loved him too much to want him tainted in some way by me. But whether a "natural" or not, I was a mum, and there had to be some way through.

If I look back now, I can see that I need not have worried

so much. Yes, Harvey is probably more sensitive to my mood than other children might be, despite me trying not to show him the worst of my depression, but he's also a wonderful little boy. The trials of the last year, whether it be my depression, his inability to communicate as much as he wants and the resulting frustration, the tantrums or his desire to assert his independence... all these we have worked through together.

In the absence of instinct, we used trial and error to find our way. In the absence of knowledge, I listened to him and did my best to find out how to work with him. After all, you can't win an argument with a two-year-old, they simply don't reason like we do. And in the absence of strength, we used love, and everything was alright.

The terrible twos were, perhaps, still terrible in their way. Yet they also taught me a great deal about our little family. I have learnt that my greatest ally in fighting the terrible twos is my son himself.

He doesn't really want to throw tantrums or get angry and frustrated, and now knows to let me help him through these times. And when the depression has dragged me lower than I ever cared to go, he has been a huge comfort, ready with either a cuddle or some game to bring me back to the real world.

He has taught me to be kinder to myself. Even allowing for parental pride, I have a very special little boy, and he's special – at least in part – because of me.

From fear and despair at my discovery I wasn't a natural mother, he has taught me it doesn't matter. With love and understanding I can learn to be a good mother, and that knowledge is the greatest gift anyone could have given me. ...which is what has made the terrible twos the best part of motherhood yet.

Chapter 11

Epilogue: Ten Toddlers Later

By Ann Marie Dwyer

Most mothers buy shoes and a new wardrobe, or get plastic surgery and a tattoo, for their mid-life crisis. Having never been part of the normal crowd, I had more children. So, as my friends are enjoying their emptying nests and my older children are battling wills with tenured college professors and toddlers of their own, my house is alive with the ever-present pitter-patter of toddler feet.

Throughout these pages, you have heard the profession of the similarity between teenagers and toddlers. Since I have them simultaneously, I am speaking from the present rather than my memories. They are so very alike.

You can likely remember your teenage years with a cryptic smile or rolled eyes. That memory qualifies you for understanding your toddler. Just as teens discover the adult world, toddlers are discovering the world, period. Their communication deficiency is not as pronounced as you might think. Try talking to a teenager...a completely foreign language. Put toddlers and teenagers in the same room, and they will carry on a conversion you will swear needs subtitles.

In short, toddlers are individuals. They are diminutive only in stature. Their spirits are large. They have the ability to show you amazing things, to force you to look at yourself and to exhibit unabashed happiness at the most elementary level.

Willful children, especially toddlers, can convince you there are more than twenty four hours in a day. Otherwise, how could your child have gone to Mother's Day Out, taken a nap, played in the yard, destroyed the carpet with spaghetti, flooded the bathroom, brushed the cat's teeth and still been able to hear three renditions of *Goodnight, Moon*? A typical day with a Terrible Two feels like a forty-eight hour root canal.

So, how is it I have survived so many times? Indeed, there is some practical advice I am compelled to share with you in a sincere desire to preserve your hair color, fingernails and psychiatry budget.

Choose your battles.

Learning is necessarily a revolution. Old ideas are shed, and new ones replace them. Your toddler has enough turmoil struggling with concepts and the expanse of knowledge he is amassing in his mental encyclopedia. Stick to your guns when it comes to safety, health, nutrition and the bright line between right and wrong.

Everything else is up for negotiation. Everything.

You know you are in trouble when your toddler tells you it is almost impossible to flush a grapefruit down the toilet. But for everything else, you have a washing machine, unfettered access to a store to replace worldly possessions, home owner's insurance and oxygen action crystals. Enjoy the easy-to-clean messes. This time is truly precious and short.

Get your hands dirty.

Exposure offers learning. When he asks how something works, explain it to him, better still: show him. If she wants to know about animals, take her to a farm or a zoo. When he wants to know how snow works, make snow cones.

Adults learn first by listening and reading. Your toddler does not communicate well enough verbally for this to be a viable option. If he cannot speak them, chances are good he cannot read the words either. Adapt to his level and learning style.

Get your fingers in the paint. Build sand castles. Hop through rain puddles. Make "yard soup". Don a shaving cream beard. Wear character make up and costumes. They are only this age once. Make the most of it by embracing your inner child.

Open your eyes.

Your child is looking through 100% clear lenses. She is not jaded by cynicism, sarcasm, failure or heartbreak. She is filled with wonder, excitement and passion. Let go of your fears, inhibitions and preconceptions.

When she brings you a leaf, look at it like she does. You have a lot to learn, not just about her, but about the world surrounding you which has disappeared into the background behind work, parenthood, responsibility and life. Share the road of discovery with her. It will keep you young.

Stop worrying.

All worry does is burn Vitamin C and make wrinkles. Stop supporting Oil of Olay.

Engage your toddler's natural lack of fear. Children are rubber until they are four, and if you don't tell them, they never outgrow it. Yes, protect him from the iron and the stove. Don't panic when he climbs on the doghouse and pretends he is flying like Superman.

It will happen.

There is no sense rushing toddlers to do much of anything. They are not the most patient animals on the planet. Since your child does not have the virtue, you must.

Every guideline you ever read is just that...a guideline. It is not the be-all-end-all authority of what your child must do, and when, to be healthy and perfectly beautiful. If the nagging worry will not subside, consult a professional: pediatrician, dietitian, dentist or psychiatrist.

If you have not had marathon training, don't worry...you will get it chasing after her in her flight from anything you really want from her. It is perfectly fine that your neighbor's child was talking three months ago and your best friend's child is already potty trained. Your child will, too...but not one second before she is ready.

Laugh at yourself.

If you have not made a dog pile on the living room floor, a giggling mass of arms and legs, you need to lighten up. Your toddler laughs at himself, and so should you laugh at yourself. Laughter is good medicine, even when you aren't sick.

Write it down.

Before you know it, she is going to be sitting on the couch with a scared, acne-afflicted man-child, whose sole purpose in life is surviving talking to her father. This will be the perfect time to tell him about the darling things she did and said at this age.

And if you can't remember but one thing from this book, let this be a mantra: Never argue with a toddler. It would be a crying shame to lose.

Credits

Without the help of some very special and talented people this book would not have come to you. I want to take a moment to thank them for their support and efforts.

Russell, my adored late husband, for long hours of keeping the children Velcroed to the yard so I could keep company with the computer to write and rewrite.

Barbara Whitlock, my dear friend, for her contributions and her kindred spirit. She is a mother in the truest sense of the word.

John McDevitt, my partner in crime, for his contributions and editorial expertise. He kept me in the margins and on topic for the most part.

Tina Hartley, my hardheaded cub, for her contributions and indomitable spirit. She reminds me everyday how easy it is to accomplish anything when someone believes in you.

Melanie Denyer, my sweet friend, for her contributions and buoyant spirit. She lets me know in the throes of a tantrum it is possible to remain calm.

Linda Valentine-Dean, my sister of my heart, for her tireless transfers of data in formats I despise. She marvels at the journey through this book as it unfolds, yet again, before her eyes.

Each one of you played a large part in making this book a reality. I thank you from the bottom of my heart.

About the Author

Ann Marie "Red" Dwyer is first and foremost a mother. After that, her titles in order of importance are grandmother, daughter, sister, friend. She occupies her time, not otherwise consumed by family, freelance writing. At the time of the publishing of this book, she is finishing her second fiction novel, a book of poetry and a parenting book on grieving the loss of a newborn.

She lives with and homeschools her autistic, mid-life crisis toddlers in South Carolina. She blogs incessantly at M3 - Momma's Money Matters about blogging, psychology, parenting and money...good advice delivered with a bit of snark and humor...and the occasional poem.

She supports the South Carolina Autism Society and encourages everyone to contribute to autism research. You could be the missing piece to the autism puzzle.

Made in the USA
Lexington, KY
01 October 2013